Your Power Path to Freedom, Success and Happiness

(Text and Workbook)

from YourBodySoulandProsperity.com

Tom Marcoux

Executive Coach

Spoken Word Strategist

Speaker-Author of 28 books

A QuickBreakthrough Publishing Edition

More copies are available from the publisher with the imprint QuickBreakthrough Publishing. For more information about this book contact: tomsupercoach@gmail.com

This book was developed and written with care. Names and details were modified to respect privacy.

Other Books by Tom Marcoux:

- Be Heard and Be Trusted: How to Get What You Want
- Nothing Can Stop You This Year!
- Darkest Secrets of Persuasion and Seduction Masters
- Darkest Secrets of Charisma
- Darkest Secrets of Negotiation Masters
- Darkest Secrets of the Film and Television Industry Every Actor Should Know
- Darkest Secrets of Making a Pitch to the Film and Television Industry
- Darkest Secrets of Film Directing
- Now You See Me – Make a Great First Impression - Networking

Praise for *Your Power Path to Freedom, Success and Happiness* and Tom Marcoux:

• "In *Your Power Path to Freedom, Success and Happiness*, you experience the powerful 'Insight—>Intuition—>Action' process. You learn to make new breakthroughs to feel good, get more done, believe in yourself and enjoy each day. Feel your personal energy increase!" – Dr. JoAnn Dahlkoetter, author, *Your Performing Edge* and Coach to CEOs and Olympic Gold Medalists

• "Tom Marcoux has distinguished himself as a coach, speaker and self-help author. His books combine his own philosophy and teachings, as well as those of other success experts, in a highly readable and relatable manner." – Danek S. Kaus, co-author of *Power Persuasion*

Praise for Tom Marcoux's Other Work:

• "In Tom Marcoux's *Now You See Me*, the powerful and easy-to-use ideas can make a big difference in your business and your personal relationships." – Allen Klein, author of *You Can't Ruin My Day*

• "Marcoux's book *10 Seconds to Wealth* focuses on how each of us have divine gifts that we need to understand and use to be our best when the crucial '10 seconds' occur.... He identifies the divine gifts and shares how these gifts can help us create what we want in our lives, and the wealth we want." – Linda Finkle, author of *Finding The Fork In The Road: The Art of Maximizing the Potential of Business Partnerships*

• "In *Darkest Secrets of Persuasion and Seduction Masters: How to Protect Yourself and Turn the Power to Good*, learn useful countermeasures to protect you from being darkly manipulated." – David Barron, co-author, *Power Persuasion*

• "In *Be Heard and Be Trusted*, Tom's advice on how to remain true to yourself and establish authentic rapport with clients is both insightful and reality based. He [shows how] to establish oneself as a credible expert." - Arthur P. Ciaramicoli, Ed.D., Ph.D., author *The Curse of the Capable*

• "In *Reduce Clutter, Enlarge Your Life*, Marcoux will help you get rid of the physical and mental clutter occupying precious space in your life. You'll reclaim wasted energy, lower your stress, and find time for new opportunities." – Laura Stack, author of *Execution IS the Strategy*

Visit Tom's blog: www.BeHeardandBeTrusted.com

Tom Marcoux

CONTENTS*

* This book includes even more material.

DEDICATION AND ACKNOWLEDGEMENTS

This book is dedicated to the terrific book and film consultant, and author Johanna E. Mac Leod. It is also dedicated to the other team members. Thanks to Barry Adamson II and David MacDowell Blue for editing certain sections. Thanks to Johanna E. MacLeod for rendering the front cover and back cover. Thanks to my father, Al Marcoux, for his concern and efforts for me. Thanks to my mother, Sumiyo Marcoux, a kind, generous soul. Thank you to Higher Power. Thanks to our readers, audiences, clients, my graduate/college students and my team members of Tom Marcoux Media, LLC.
The best to you.

DISCOVER THE SECRET OF "INSIGHT—>INTUITION—>ACTION"

You want more and better in your life, right?

More Success. More opportunities. Better relationships. More happy moments—yes?

Use this book as your springboard to a better life.

Imagine stepping forward on your personalized *Power Path to Freedom, Success and Happiness.*

For example, my client Serena wanted to give a speech to a major organization in San Francisco. This was a big opportunity for her, but she was shutting down emotionally. She came to me to guide her to express herself well and gain confidence.

To set her on her Power Path, I asked Serena powerful questions, and she became clear on her personal values and what she could express from her heart.

As she stepped up to the podium, her right hand trembled. But when she expressed her heartfelt values, she could feel the audience warm up to her. They were attentive. In response to Serena's humor, their laughter rocked the room.

The speech proved a success! Serena had discovered

something new in herself.

She found the *Keys to Success* that include knowing yourself, expanding your actions, and expressing what's in your heart.

As an Executive Coach, I help my clients take their lives to higher levels of success and happiness.

I've helped clients prepare for auditions/interviews, build a brand, take a blog from zero to visitors from 141 countries, write a first book, start a business, lead a team, and more.

Now through this book, I serve as your Executive Coach.

This Book Helps You Leap Forward for More Success and Happiness:

My work involves helping clients connect with their intuition.

I use questions and my clients experience this powerful process:

Insight—>Intuition—>Action.

With this pattern, my clients have an experience of what I call *Catapult-Moments*. The catapult on an aircraft carrier kicks the plane forward fast. With Catapult-Moments, you jump forward. You find something new and better. You experience extraordinary progress. Clarity arrives and you feel so alive!

Part of this process helps you **develop skills, strength and stamina**—all vital elements for *Your Power Path*.

I am truly happy to share with you insights and methods under the headings:

- Stop Giving Your Power Away!
- Don't Let Fear Shut Down Your Creativity
- Love Yourself to Financial Abundance
- Love Yourself to Spiritual Joy
- Move Ahead Successfully Even When You're

Criticized

- and many others . . .

These sections are designed so you can connect with the material and quickly answer related questions.

I use certain phrases so people understand them and remember the ideas. For example, as I coach CEOs, business owners and others, I express my phrase: *"Take command, Focus Your Brand."* Even if you don't have a business, you have a personal brand (it is what you're best known for). Your clarity makes it possible to get more of what you want in life.

Know that answering the provided questions even for just 20 seconds will give you a surprising advantage: You'll learn more about yourself and how to improve your daily actions and strategies in achieving success for your life.

Let's take the next step.

USE A "MIRACLE MOMENT" TO OVERCOME YOUR FEAR AND ACHIEVE YOUR DREAM!

As I walked on the ocean floor, I took a deep breath and smiled. This was accomplishing one of my Big Dreams.

As a boy, I was thrilled by watching the Disney live-action feature film *20,000 Leagues Under the Sea*. I saw a team of men walking on the bottom of the ocean.

Later, I enjoyed James Cameron's film *The Abyss* which also included deep sea divers.

To get to the point of walking on the floor of the ocean, I had to *overcome two fears* related to *Sharks!* and to the claustrophobia of wearing a diving helmet.

Some days before my trip to the Grand Caymans, I practiced wearing a hood and visualizing that I was fine while wearing the helmet and walking on the ocean floor. *Positive visualization helped.*

I also asked about the presence of sharks, and I was informed that where I was diving sharks found the noise of various ships and the busy port to be off-putting.

Here's what I call the "Miracle Moment" to Really Achieve Your Dream:

It's the moment you connect with Something More Important than Your Fear.

Fulfilling my dream of walking on the ocean's floor was more important to me than my fear.

"Courage is not the absence of fear but rather the judgment that something is more important than fear." – Meg Cabot

Now it's your turn.

Write down your answers to these questions:

What is your Big Dream?

_____

_____

_____

What do you want to do?

_____

_____

What will *Feel Great!* to *you* as you're accomplishing your Big Dream?

_____

_____

_____

What will you be able to do that you cannot do now— when you accomplish your Big Dream?

_____

_____

_____

What fears are connected to what you need to do to accomplish your Big Dream?

_____

_____

_____

What about your Big Dream is More Important than Your Fear?

The above process is connected to what you want *to feel* when you're realizing your dream.

As an Executive Coach, I often help clients move beyond their comfort zone and to accomplish extraordinary things. I help my clients connect with Big Energy (which is heartfelt) and then they have something More Important than their fear.

Take the time to really connect with what moves your heart. Then, from this foundation, spring up and make progress to accomplish your dream.

LOVE YOURSELF TO SPIRITUAL JOY

Have you ever been cut down by a friend or family member and just wanted to shake off the pain and get on with your life? We'll explore three truths that will nurture you.

1. Spiritual Joy is in this present moment.

Earlier today, I went to see my father and mother. They live in another city some distance from me. My mother is a kind, generous soul, and I wonder how she got burdened by my father who seems to become bitter to a greater degree with each passing year.

My sweetheart proclaimed today that she never wants to be in the presence of my father again.

I can empathize with that.

The rude and mean comments that my father said today remind me that Spiritual Joy is in this present moment. How?

My interaction with my father is *in the past.*

I have a choice right now as to what I do. Sure a painful thought may arise; **my choice is in my *next* thought.** So I now choose to have better moments as I write this section. I find comfort and insight as I write. I also find meaning in sharing helpful ideas with my readers. Before today, I had expected to complete and post a different article. But now this section (also posted as an article) feels relevant and timely.

We have a choice with each moment: To make the most of this moment or to get lost in pain or regret of the past. Or to be twisted by worries for the future. Either way, we step out of the present moment.

You see my father's cut-down remarks of today echo how he'd throw me into walls when I was a boy.

The difference is that *as a man I now chose to end the conversation.* When his remarks were too much, I simply said, "We're done," and I stepped away from him. My father left the building.

I chose my next moment. Away from my father, I sat with my sweetheart and my mother and we had some good moments together.

2. Become skilled to *return* to the present moment.

Many spiritual paths emphasize deep breathing, prayer or quiet time to bring us into the present moment.

As I write these words, I take deep breaths, allowing my belly to expand on inhaling. I exhale and allow my belly to deflate.

Try three such breaths now, and see how you start to feel more calm.

Another method of returning to the present moment is embodied in the phrase: "I don't run that show." I use this phrase to remind myself that there is much I do not control. I do not control my father's bitterness. I do not control that my kind mother is married to someone who routinely says to her and me, "You make me mad."

An old phrase is: "You teach people how to treat you." Today, I ended a conversation in which my father berated me. That may or may not help.

I make choices as best as I can. And still, "I don't run that show."

Why is it important to return to the present moment? It's where you can experience joy. Also, if you're clear of past pain, you can respond to opportunities in the present moment.

When you answer the knock of opportunity, you need your bags already packed. – Tom Marcoux

3. Compassion is the answer.

Some definitions of compassion include "recognizing another's pain with the desire to relieve it."

Imagine that you truly love yourself. What would that mean?

Would you allow yourself to be imperfect?

I'll put this another way. What would you say to your best friend if he or she was going through a difficulty?

Wouldn't you be kind? Wouldn't you suggest that your friend take care of himself or herself?

Sure you would.

I'm inviting you to look upon your own pain with compassion.

Give yourself what you need.

Further, I invite you to explore how you release yourself from painful feelings. *Forgiveness actually frees the person who forgives.*

I choose at this time to avoid cutting off interaction with my father.

The next time I see him he may address me with berating words—or not.

I'll see what happens when I get there.

I call this "enter the moment fresh."

When I see my father the next time, will I respond to his berating words with "We're done" or will I listen for a time?

I'll enter the moment fresh.

And I'll remember that compassion toward myself and to others will be a helpful guideline.

Compassion helps us experience spiritual joy.

As an Executive Coach, I help my clients develop skills, strength and stamina. It's vital to learn to take good care of ourselves.

(By the way, the above section is one I wrote some time ago. I am glad that in later interactions with my father that I had the *strength* to listen to him, to hear him out. He still had an edge to some of his words, but he had some okay comments, too. Some men do not age gracefully. As they lose things in their lives (my father lost his ability to go running), some men fail to flow forward. I advocate that we do not stand for abuse. Still, there are times to show compassion. Showing compassion takes real personal energy. *Take good care of yourself.* Many blessings on your journey.)

Now it's your turn.

How will you chose to *return* to the present moment?

(Will you say a prayer of gratitude? Will you practice deep breathing? Will you choose to close abusive conversations?

_____

_____

_____

_____

_____

_____

_____

_____

How will you show compassion toward yourself?

(Will you give yourself more breaks to refresh yourself? Will you take a class that energizes you? Will you get time away and soak in a hot bath?)

_____

_____

_____

_____

_____

_____

_____

_____

_____

BE GOOD TO YOUR BODY –
THE P.O.W.E.R. PROCESS

I first shared this material in my book *I Left My Thighs in San Francisco: How You Can Use a New Time-Saving System for Weight Loss, Exercise, More Energy, and Being Happy While You Drop Weight.*

We'll begin with the **P.O.W.E.R.** process:
P – Power-up "10"
O – organize Top Six Targets
W – work the strategy for exercise
E – engage the Trigger-Set Method
R – rig a "success system" and drop "perfectionism-pain"

1. Power-up "10"
To start developing your fitness, especially when you're busy, consider *"The Power of 10"* which I also call the *"Mighty Minimum."*

For example, when I was directing a feature film, the Power of 10 meant to me:

- 10 palm strikes
- 10 front kicks
- 10 side kicks
- 10 sit-ups
- 10 pushups
- 10 oblique sit-ups

Doing the above exercises might take only five minutes, and still, this process is working several major muscle groups.

The Power of 10 can be applied to weight training, too.

One does **10 lifting moves per arm** for a total of 20.

- 20 bicep curls
- 20 forward lifts for part of the shoulder
- 20 sideways lifts for another part of the shoulder
- 20 leaning over lifts for another part of the shoulder
- 20 triceps-related lifts
- 20 forearms-related lifts.

The above weight training can be done in five minutes or less.

CAUTION: Consult a doctor about your own fitness level when considering any exercise regimen.

The Power of 10 can apply to 10 minutes on the treadmill. The Big Benefit is that at 10 minutes, it often feels like "That was easy." This means that you won't dread tomorrow's 10 minutes on the treadmill.

The Power of 10 relates to what I call the *Mighty Minimum*. Imagine that you do a minimum of 10 sit-ups a day. That's 300 per month and 3,600 sit-ups per year—a real gain in core strength. In a way, we can say the minimum number of sit-ups makes you "mighty."

This reminds me of a quote from Joss Whedon's TV show

Firefly: "We've done the impossible, and that makes us mighty."

A side note: One of my editors said that this "Power of 10" seems "too easy." I replied, "I'm looking for daily progress. I emphasize *better than zero.* After a good start, any individual can pursue expanding their exercise regimen in ways that apply to their individual needs."

2. Organize *Top Six Targets*

Just before you go to sleep, consider writing your *Top Six Targets*—the most important tasks for your next day. Each week, I write "weights" a few times as one of my Top Six Targets for the next day. With Top Six Targets, you identify what will make your day successful. Addressing audiences, I say, "2 for you, 2 for family, and 2 for work." This is a great method for prioritizing, and it gives you "marching orders" so you get into action faster the next day.

3. Work the strategy for exercise

Focus on *keep moving.* Research has shown that thinner people simply move more than heavier people. They walk up and down stairs, and even some twitch their foot when sitting. When I say "work the strategy for exercise," I mean work in exercise throughout the day. For example, during a break, I take the stairs when I'm on campus where I teach college students.

The strategy of "keep moving" works for entering your home to begin exercise so you step straight over to your treadmill.

One of my clients closes the door and (as she tells me) exercises in her underwear for "10 Terrific Minutes."

To get more out of her 10 minutes on the treadmill, she has the front of the treadmill raised so her session is all "walking uphill."

4. Engage the *Trigger-Set Method*

Everyday, you and I react to triggers. How? Imagine you like cookies and your family member leaves them out on the living room table. Will you eat a cookie? Many people reply: "Probably." The real answer is often "Yes!"

What's the solution? Place the cookies into the cupboard where you cannot see them. This way the negative trigger of seeing the cookies does *not* happen.

Here's another strategy about triggers:

"Set the Positive Trigger when the situation is COOL –

So you automatically do the positive action when the situation is HOT."

For example, I have a positive trigger in my bedroom: a treadmill that is clear of anything on it.

With audiences, I often observe, "Do you have stationary bicycle? Yes—it's the most expensive towel rack."

So be strategic. Set up a positive trigger and avoid clogging it with towels!

5. Rig a "success system" and drop "perfectionism-pain"

We can effectively develop and use a *success system* when we identify what we most want and create an incremental way to achieve it.

Still, for many of us, a stumbling block is what I call *Perfectionism-Pain*—which often arises from *comparison*. If you compare yourself to professional athletes, actors, and actresses related to appearance, then such thoughts of trying to *compete* can send you into a downward, negative spiral. This creates real pain.

For the most part, this book is *not* designed for the professional athlete nor some young, genetically-gifted, stereotypically attractive person.

You might notice my choice of the above words.

For example, at this moment, I have gray hair at my temples. I am NOT trying to look younger than I am. Sure, I have footage of myself starring in a feature film when I was in my 20's. I don't watch it. *I own who I am today.*

In essence, I do NOT compete with my younger self.

My point is: *Drop Perfectionism-Pain.* Avoid trying to look perfect like a professional athlete or professional actor/actress.

Instead, pick your own goals to be a great version of *Yourself.*

I often say, "Don't compete, *connect.*"

Connect with your own heartfelt goals. *Many of us realize that we really want to be fit and healthy.* Also, for many of us, being healthy means dropping excess belly fat but we do not need six pack abs.

One of my friends, Joe, when he was a model achieved six pack abs. I asked him how he did it. "I eat soups," was his quick response.

So Joe was willing to pay the price for his six pack abs. After all, his appearance *was* his profession.

In this book, we're talking about *integrating* exercise into your busy life.

So what do we do when a "perfectionism thought" arises? Here are examples my clients have mentioned:

Perfectionism Thoughts:

- "Oh, look at her. She's got buns of steel. I've got buns of cellulite."
- "Oh, look at that guy. He could wear a Superman outfit. I could wear a whale outfit."

Perfectionism Thoughts are all about comparison. Shift

your thoughts *to what you are doing for your health.*

The strategy is to shift from a Perfectionism Thought to what I call *"The Empowering Second Thought."* It really helps to condition yourself to have an instant, empowering response when a negative thought arises.

Stephen's pattern is this:

Perfectionism Thought: "Oh, look at that guy. He could wear a Superman outfit. I could wear a whale outfit."

Empowering Second Thought: "I'm making progress. I'm five pounds closer to my goal, and I am walking right now!"

Now, we'll continue building your Success System.

The Elements of a "Success System":

To set a habit takes more than 30 days. Why? Because once we get to the 30 day mark, many of us relax our vigilance and indulge in some diet-busting behavior. Some authors suggest that habit-building may take 40 days. In any case, we can use strategies to build our empowering habits. We'll use the C.A.N. process:

C – connects to your current activities

A – automatically-works

N – nurtures your feelings

Connects to your current activities. It helps to "attach" a new behavior to something you already naturally do. I read every day so a good plan is for me to read and walk on a treadmill. The added benefit is that reading makes the time go by pleasantly while I'm on the treadmill.

Automatically-works. By this I mean that you set up an automatic, positive behavior. Researchers talk about the benefits of positive habits. The idea is that you only make the decision once and then you automatically carry it out.

For example, my sweetheart and I set up an *automatic behavior*. After dinner and the dishes are in the dish washing machine, she and I immediately leave for our evening walk and conversation. There is no hesitation. We do not make a new decision. We automatically take action.

Nurtures your feelings. We do so much just to get a good feeling. Why do people drink soda? It's an enjoyable experience. See if you can develop your exercise routine so that you enjoy some good experiences. I like talking with my sweetheart so it's great that we can combine our conversation with an evening walk.

For more about our feelings . . .

A Brief Discussion about Addiction

"I'm addicted to chocolate," my friend Anne said with enthusiasm. Is that true?

Dr. Michael F Roizen wrote: "When we talk about addiction circuitry, it comes down to these factors: a) If the behavior has a beneficial effect in the short term but adverse consequences in the long term, b) if the person develops a tolerance . . . and then needs more and more…, and c) if the person experiences symptoms of withdrawal…when he or she tries to stop doing the behavior."

For many of us the short term benefit is a rise in dopamine and endorphins (the feel-good substances in the body). Some of us get a rush of good feelings from a donut or ice cream. Our brain makes a connection: "I want to feel good so I'll get more donuts!"

To change our behavior is often more than a simple dropping of a bad habit. We often need to learn to replace the habit with something that helps us feel better.

Serena replaced a donut with an orange and dancing around (when at home alone) to her favorite invigorating music. She has strategically replaced eating a donut with another behavior that helps her feel good—and fast!

I often write about: **"Set the Positive Trigger when the situation is COOL—so you automatically take action when the situation is HOT."**

For Serena, the "hot" situation is arriving home after work. She's tired and she wants a treat. It takes well-considered strategy to replace reflexive-eating behaviors.

Other details about addiction (alcohol, drugs, etc.) are beyond the scope of this book.

Still it is valuable to examine your own behaviors and see if you appear to have some addictive patterns.

My point is that setting a Success System and being aware of any perfectionism thoughts helps you stay consistent with your Drop-Weight Plan.

What is a situation that can cause problems for your weight loss plans? How can you set a Positive Trigger when the situation is COOL? What will your Positive Trigger be? How can you use it when the situation is HOT?

_____

_____

_____

_____

_____

_____

_____

_____

_____

_____

_____

_____

THE TRUTH ON HOW YOU CAN KEEP GOING WHILE OTHERS QUIT

The tension at the table in the restaurant felt like a smothering blanket. My former business associate looked at me with barely contained anger. Things had not gone well. We had learned the hard way that we were not a match for working on a project together. The resulting impasse had cost months of paperwork.

I reached over for a napkin, and my suit sleeve caught on my water glass. Then it was like time stopped for a moment. My water glass balanced on its edge, then SPLASH—water spilled all over the table.

Amazing! That was just the thing to dispel the tension. And the matter between us was ultimately resolved. It began with a suit sleeve and a glass of water.

When you're working on projects that are long term and mean so much to you, you're likely to meet with resistance. The Big Goals often include big obstacles, and we need strategies to help us carry on.

A certain few people will **make this year a great year** for themselves. Many others will quit. But not you—when you apply the following strategies embodied in the N.E.W. process:

N – nurture Levels of Goals
E – energize through new ideas/skills
W – work the Worst First cure to procrastination

1. Nurture Levels of Goals

Whether you keep going or quit depends on your skills to use your emotion to energize your continued progress.

By this I mean, your emotion, properly channeled, can help you endure and ultimately fulfill your Big Goal.

A lot of people quit when their positive feeling (like "Oh! I look forward to being 40 pounds lighter") fizzles out.

To really be sure to keep going, it helps to have multiple Levels of Goals.

I'm talking about not just relying on "positive motivation." Instead, use whatever works!

The solution is to use 3 Emotional Focus-Points:

3 Emotional Focus-Points:
- Golden Pull Goals
- Dark Boot Goals
- Green Tranquility Goals

Let's tackle the *Golden Pull Goal* (positive goal) of getting more sales. Sure, that's a positive thing. You might even make a plan to give yourself a personal reward when you accomplish more sales.

However, many of us realize that what really pushes us forward is a *Dark Boot Goal*. It's like a boot that kicks us in the rear end. In this situation, a Dark Boot Goal would be "*avoid* having to tell my wife that our vacation is cancelled because I failed to sell enough widgets." You work hard to make sure what you fear does NOT happen.

Along this line, here's another powerful Dark Boot Goal: "*avoid* tax penalties by turning in my tax return on time!"

Finally, after achieving many goals, I realized that I need goals that would sustain my well-being. I call these goals *Green Tranquility Goals*. I recall hearing about a building that was built to be "green" and "self-sustaining."

We, human beings, need to be self-sustaining, too. For example, I take a walk with my sweetheart every day, and that is one of my Green Tranquility Goals. It helps me feel calm and peaceful.

So when you set a goal, be sure to set up a related Golden Pull Goal, Dark Boot Goal and Green Tranquility Goal.

2. Energize through new ideas/skills

You cannot solve a problem on the same level in which it was created. – Albert Einstein

When I was in my 20's I needed to raise funds to produce a feature film. I had no idea how to do it. And for months I really suffered because I had a dream but also had big fears and no new skills. So what did I do? I gained a number of mentors and also began reading a lot. Now, I tend to read 81 books a year.

My focus is on getting new ideas and new skills each year because I do not know what new opportunities may arise.

More than that, as an Executive Coach, I'm constantly studying new trends and methods so my clients can *Move Forward Fast.*

With my clients and graduate students, I emphasize this idea: **"You need preparation so that you're strong to face the unknowns."**

To really make sure you have the time management skills and ways to overcome procrastination, please consider my book: *Nothing Can Stop You This Year!: How to Unleash Your Hidden Power to Persuade Well, Get More Done, Gain Sudden Profits, Command Intuition and Feel Great!* (See a Free Chapter at Amazon.com).

3. Work the "Worst First cure" to procrastination

For many of us, procrastination is a habit. It's almost like a default setting. We feel that something may be unpleasant to do so we go on "automatic" and put it off.

Here's a better habit—an empowering habit: **"Worst First."** By this I mean do the Worst Task first. Here's an important observation: *The task you dread the most is the most important one for your career.*

If you're dreading updating your resume, it's probably the most important thing for you to do. [Learn more in my book, **Power Time Management:** *More Time, Less Stress, and Zero Procrastination (Your Breakthrough for More Success, Happiness and Time Off)* [See a Free Chapter on Amazon.com.]

As an Executive Coach, I see that some of my clients dread marketing and, of course, many of them would *do the best thing for their business* by getting help to do better marketing. This section first appeared in my blog YourBodySoulandProsperity.com—and I know that we can eliminate blocks to the flow of more prosperity in our life. Sometimes the *Worst First Task* (to bring more prosperity) is: **Start the process of getting help**. Perhaps, you need to interview three people to find a marketing consultant or business coach.

Maybe you *are* a business coach, and you need to help people learn about what you do. **So maybe your Worst First Task is to make a 1 minute video** for YouTube.com. (People often prefer to see a 1 minute video than to read a blog page.) Here's an example: I made a 1.7 minute video that pulls back the curtain so you see how directing a feature film that went to the Cannes Film market and training Stanford University MBA students all add up for how I help people rise to higher levels of Real Success. On YouTube.com, type: "Build Your Brand Tom Marcoux."

Personally, I dread doing certain paperwork. How do I handle it? I work on it first thing in the morning. 15 minutes a day adds up when you do the Worst First task consistently.

Observe yourself. When do you have energy? When you wake up? Or later in the day? Or are you a night owl?

One of my clients writes from 5 pm – 6 pm because he has a "second wind" at that time.

Use your best energy to apply to your Worst First task.

One college professor cleared his apartment of clutter by using the first 15 minutes of each day to clear clutter and straighten up. Soon his living quarters were in great shape.

Now it's your turn.

What do you want to improve for this year?

Identify your Worst First task and get going.

Make this year an outstanding year for yourself. Apply the N.E.W. process:

N – nurture Levels of Goals

E – energize through new ideas/skills

W – work the "Worst First cure" to procrastination

You deserve to live the life of your dreams.
It begins today.

What is your Worst First task? How can your life improve once you accomplish this particular Worst First task? How will you reward yourself for accomplishing this task? Can you get help on this task? When are you fresh during the day so you have great energy to apply to you Worst First task?

EXPERIENCE "INNER PEACE IN A MOMENT"

Do you really want success? Then you need to be at your best in crucial moments. How do you accomplish that? You learn to guard your personal energy. Here is the process of "Inner Peace in a Moment" as we use the Y.E.S. techniques:

Y – yield with "I don't run that show"
E – encourage with "It was a good run."
S – smile with "It is as it is."

1. Yield with "I don't run that show"

To guard your energy, learn when to stop trying to control everything. How much do you control anyway? Do you control your mother's opinion of your friends? I didn't think so.

One way to conserve your personal energy is to *use this phrase "I don't run that show" to shift your thoughts.*

Let's say your mother does not like your friends: Tell yourself "I don't run that show."

You go to a store where clerks ignore customers . . . *I don't run that show.*

(And you can turn on your heel and leave the store.)

The phrase "I don't run that show" can *free up* so much of your energy!

2. Encourage with "It was a good run."

You can encourage yourself even if you're losing something precious. When you say, "it was a good run," you're expressing gratitude for something that you enjoyed. You're also reminding yourself that you are entering a *new chapter of life,* and there will be *new things* that will "have a good run."

Also you're *not* pushing against the universe. Things come and go. No matter how we protest, some things fade away. Guard your energy. Devote your attention to what is *now blossoming in your life.*

As an Executive Coach, I help my clients shift from dis-empowering feelings to empowering ones that make it easy for them to do **new and better actions.**

Things run their course.

Yes, I'm sad that there is only one season of the TV show *Firefly.* Still, it was a great season . . . so I say, "It was a good run."

Several years ago, I worked with a good group of people. We set up the first bank with online banking and then the bank abruptly laid off 30 people—all of us. Ouch! That hurt... **It was a good run.**

"To offer no resistance to life is to be in a state of grace, ease and lightness." – Eckhart Tolle

3. Smile with "It is as it is."

I have an elderly relative who can say plain mean things.

One day I surprised myself and my relative. He said something awful, and I simply laughed and said, "Well, *that* was something to shake things up!"

He knew what he was doing. He attempted to make me "wrong" and press upon me that I never measure up to his opinion.

Instead of taking offense, I laughed. I'm not suggesting that laughter is always the best response. In fact, sometimes, laughing does NOT help.

Still, my point is: in that moment when I smiled, I was NOT going into the hole of feeling bad. How? I was non-attached to proving any point. I was non-attached to straightening this person out. He simply is set in his ways.

Instead, I had a better experience in that I had **a feeling of calm when I told myself: "It is as it is."**

I learned about the power of "It is as it is" when I was 15 years old. I was learning about unconditional love and a tough realization hit me: my father was incapable of expressing unconditional love to me. He had rules, and "that's it." Here is a man who dropped many friends because they "did not measure up." In fact, now decades later he has only one friend.

So at 15 years old, I could feel it. I was slipping towards bitterness about my father's coldness or *I could make another choice.* So I went to the level of healthy acceptance and "it is as it is."

My father had already tied up his thinking, and he was not interested in learning from anyone let alone his own son. This attitude in my father continues to this day. It's sad, really. At this point, my sweetheart refuses to be in the same building with my father. When I visit, she goes to a nearby coffee shop. And I understand her point of view.

I look at the patterns of my father, and *I simply free my own energy when I say, "It is as it is."*

* * *

To experience *Inner Peace in a Moment*, make efforts to condition yourself to have these three phrases readily available in your mind:

3 Phrases of Inner Peace in a Moment
- I don't run that show.
- It was a good run.
- It is as it is.

This is *not* about giving up.

This is about *consciously choosing* where you put your mental energy and focus.

Some things in life do *not* deserve your energy. As an Executive Coach, I help my client focus on what the next and best action is. We get the obstacles out of the way.

Now, let's talk about *what deserves your focus and energy:* I remember a moment when I felt connected with the universe. One Holiday Season, I was wrapping a Christmas gift for my then-girlfriend. I was *not* searching for love. I was *not* anticipating something in return. In that moment, I had connected with the experience of *being love.*

When you practice the *3 Phrases of Inner Peace in a Moment*, you can have more calm and harmonious moments. You can simply *be* calm and in harmony.

What is a situation that really disrupts your inner peace? Which of the phrases ("I don't run that show; It was good run; It is as it is") would help you shift your mood into a positive direction? . . . Write down some other phrases of

your own that will help you make the positive shift in
your mood.

_____

_____

_____

_____

_____

_____

_____

_____

GET STRONG, FACE RISK AND ACHIEVE YOUR DREAM

"I'm afraid," my client Sharon said. "I can help you with that. I'll introduce you to the process of 'Bring the Safety Net Up With You," I replied. We'll use the N.E.T. process:

N – nurture your resources
E – expand your plan
T – target the purpose

Several years ago, one of my clients said, "I'm afraid. The higher I rise, the further I have to fall."

I replied, "We'll find ways to bring your safety net up with you."

1. Nurture your resources.

"Nothing is impossible for the [person] who doesn't have to do it himself." – A. H. Weiler

Facing risk can be a scary time. It's vital for you to look at all your current resources and to find even more resources. You do *not* have to step forward by yourself.

It is helpful to develop relationships with excellent professionals before you need them.

For example, I went looking for an entertainment industry attorney before I needed her to work on projects that I was going to do in subsequent years.

Barbra Streisand, at the beginning of her career, was helped by friends who let her sleep on their couch.

Now it's your turn.

Answer these questions:

- Who can help you?
- Which professionals could assist you (attorney, accountant, financial planner, and others)?

As an Executive Coach, I often take on different roles of coach, business consultant, brand strategist, speech coach, and mentor. I currently lead teams in the United Kingdom, India and the United States of America. *I have trained with my own mentors* in leadership, top level speech-making and more.

I hire my own coaches and consultants so I'm constantly improving my strategic approach.

It helps for you to keep studying and reading. If reading is not your strong suit, consider listening to audio books. [My audio books are available on iTunes: *Be Heard and Be Trusted*—and my other audio book, *Darkest Secrets of Persuasion and Seduction Masters: How to Protect Yourself and Turn the Power to Good.*]

2. Expand your plan

To face risk in an effective manner, look at the whole situation. A number of people refer to this as "look at the whole chessboard."

Have multiple plans.

Answer these questions and write down your answers in your plans:

- What if the first phase of your project does not work? How can you recover?
- How can you minimize the damage?
- How can you go into action quickly?
- How can you keep the budget modest, so you do not risk the whole company?

The team that made $100 million with the Thighmaster product, began with a plan to develop and market eight products. The first product did not work, and Thighmaster was product #2.

Many years ago, I was flown into Utah as a finalist to be a trainer for a top time management company. It looked like the articulate, blond woman gained that position.

Sure, I was disappointed. I did not stop. Instead, I "got on another horse."

I immediately rented a church and held my own time management workshop using my own proprietary methods. The workshop started me on the path to giving six speeches at the annual conferences for the National Association of Broadcasters, Washington, D.C. And that led to my teaching graduate students and college students for 15 years.

It's great to have multiple plans.

It's like having multiple irons in the fire because you do not know which particular iron will become red hot.

Now it's your turn.

Write down an *Expanded Plan.*
Include:
- How you can recover if Phase One of your project does not work out.
- How you can fall back and do something else while your revise the project.
- How you can keep finances going as you develop your project.

I've interviewed a number of people who have successfully conducted crowdfunding campaigns.

One person I know raised his rent-money by offering to make a simple website for people who donated $100.00. A number of people took up his offer.

Many times, a money problem can be converted into a **"find another way to serve people" solution.**

3. Target the purpose

When you truly connect with your purpose for a project or your "life-direction," you can be flexible and jump at multiple opportunities.

I've learned that being out in the world and finding ways to serve others brings on more opportunities.

Many years ago, I served a group of job-seekers by giving a presentation at the San Francisco Employment Development Department. I taught skills to help people develop their effective personal brand.

My purpose was to be helpful to these people who were hurting due to enduring a job loss.

One attendee came up to me and said, "You should speak for XY company." This led to over $312,000 worth of work.

Now it's your turn.

What is your purpose?

Do you want to entertain people? Can you do it as a writer, actor, singer—or some combination?

Do you want to lift people's hearts? Can you do it by giving a speech?—revising a speech for someone else?—co-writing a book?

* * *

When you're facing a risk, see if you can pause and do some strategic planning.

Take a long view. Keep looking to expand your skills and experience.

Stay active and find ways to serve.

What do you *really* want? What is a risk that you may need to face? How can you marshal your resources? Who can help you? How can you make a strategic plan so that you're okay even if initial outcomes are disappointing or troublesome? How can you take good care of yourself so you have the strength and resiliency to carry on and eventually triumph?

_____

_____

_____

_____

_____

_____

_____

_____

_____

_____

_____

_____

DON'T HAVE ENOUGH TIME?!—WHAT YOU CAN DO FOR YOUR DREAM AND FOR BETTER RELATIONSHIPS

Imagine a time when you're running fast—from appointment to appointment, errand to errand. Work is slamming you hard with overtime. You can barely catch your breath. And you're not sleeping much. Ugh. Pain.

Here's a helpful idea: **"Better than zero."**

Do you feel that you don't have time for exercise?

At one point, my sweetheart and I visited another city and stayed at a friend's home. I got my exercise in by suggesting that we all take a walk.

Now there are some people who scoff at a walk instead of running or hitting the gym. And to that I reply: "Better than zero."

And there are times when I apply the "Power of 10" (10 pushups, 10 sit-ups, 10 palm strikes, 10 side kicks and so forth). It just takes a few minutes.

(For more about making the best of your time, see my book, *Power Time Management: More Time, Less Stress, and*

Zero Procrastination (Your Breakthrough for More Success, Happiness and Time Off)—see a Free Chapter at Amazon.com.

How about expressing your love to your romantic partner? Pick up a card while you're getting groceries. No time to get the perfect card? Pick a good card and write your own endearments to augment the message printed in the card. Don't have the words? How about reminding your loved one of good moments shared on a vacation and write: "Thank you. I treasure those moments with you. I love you."

I always remember this quote:

"We do not remember days, we remember moments."
– Cesare Pavese

How to Make Progress On Your Dream:
Do not wait for the perfect time! **See if you can grab some progress anytime you're waiting**. For example, some hours ago, I was in a recording studio working on music. While the recording engineer worked on improving the sound of each track (we use multiple tracks), I walked in the hallway. I completed 2,379 steps of my daily 10,000 steps. While I walked, I had my pen and notepad out to write notes related to my next speech.
Make progress by using "small pockets of time."

What are small pockets of time that arise in your week? How can you accomplish some bit of progress in various small pockets of time? . . . What small thing can you do (write a note, buy a small gift, make a phone call) to show someone you care about that they are important to you?

_____

_____

_____

_____

_____

_____

_____

_____

REDUCE STRESS—
YOU KNOW YOU WANT TO . . .

I'll put it in a few words: our mouths cause us so much needless stress. Let's take this further. Imagine if your personal brand included: "Good listener." (By the way, your personal brand is your answer to this question: "What are you best known for?")

What would result if people perceived you as a good listener? Many of them would feel comfortable around you, and they'd trust you. Research demonstrates that many of the best salespeople are the best listeners. To reduce stress, we'll use the L.E.S.S. process:

L – listen

E – ease up

S – select Criteria for Excellence

S – sidestep resistance

1. Listen

I have a relative who couldn't listen to another person if

his life depended on it. It's tragic really. This person misses so much of what is warm and genuine in life. And imagine what his family misses, too. This guy has only one friend. He's dropped everyone else. And they're probably saying, "Thank you. Thank you!"

On the other hand, people who listen well often find that people like them and offer them more opportunities.

The central element of listening is restraining yourself from making reactive comments. Pause. See if you can make space for the person to experience what he or she is feeling. Even saying something as simple as "That sounds frustrating," can give the person an opportunity to relax. If we do not give the other person space to be heard, then he or she feels a tension to prove the self right. You reduce stress by listening and thus eliminating such tension.

I've noticed that certain times I have felt upset as an elderly relative denied that I was under pressure. One person likes to say, "You chose that." Sure, I've chosen to run businesses, but I did not resign from the human race and eliminate feeling pressure. A simple comment like: "That sounds rough. How did things go for you?" would be helpful.

2. Ease up

Some people try too hard. You can see them straining. The best actors "make it look easy." In my book *Darkest Secrets of Making A Pitch for Film and Television* (free chapter on Amazon.com) , I write about one of my methods to relax before I give a pitch. I tell myself: "Let's see if they want to play." That's part of my process to "ease up."

The idea of "want to play" brings the interaction out of the emotional brain's perception of "life or death."

Another part of "ease up" is to relax and let the other person say what he or she needs to say first. When two people meet and talk, each one wants to express personal thoughts and feelings. When you let the other person go first, you eliminate tension. Then the person is likely to be more receptive to hearing you. This reduces stress.

3. Select Criteria for Excellence

Being a perfectionist is stressful! I know this when I try to be so compassionate and kind to everyone I meet. But sometimes I fall short because I'm distracted. There is a solution: instead of aiming for perfection, aim for excellence. What is excellence? You decide. Set up your own Criteria for Excellence. For example, I train my graduate students in my public speaking class to focus on this idea: "We do not need you to be perfect; we do need you to be genuine." When you aim to be a real human being and express some truth (at least something that is true to you), you can take some of the pressure off. You do not need to pronounce each word perfectly. You focus on talking to the audience—and not at them.

If your mind goes blank for a moment, you can say, "I'll need a moment. My brain needs more RAM." And then the audience (at least in Silicon Valley) will enjoy the human moment and the humor.

4. Sidestep resistance

Resistance and conflict cause more and more stress. What if you could avoid needless resistance? How would your life improve?

Here's the big opportunity. Add this to your personal brand: "effective storyteller." How do you avoid a lot of needless resistance? Tell a vivid, to-the-point story.

Do not start by making some biased, blanket statement. Instead, tell a story. Give the audience (which can be one co-worker or a group in a room) an experience. Tell what you learned. It helps to end your story with something like: "So that day, I learned to pay attention to the little things because they can really trip you up—if you're not careful."

You can really reduce your stress, when you focus on these four actions:

L – listen

E – ease up

S – select Criteria for Excellence

S – sidestep resistance

The best to you.

Pick an important project. How can your figure out the Criteria for Excellence? In other words, what is crucial for the success of the project? And what can you drop from the project? Do you need to consult with end users to find out what they most need from the project?

_____

_____

_____

_____

_____

_____

_____

_____

_____

_____

_____

_____

_____

MOVE AHEAD SUCCESSFULLY
EVEN WHEN YOU'RE CRITICIZED

Do you want real success and fulfillment? Then, learn to handle criticism in an empowered manner. The crucial detail when facing criticism is to prepare to answer your own personal and empowering questions.

1. Does this person really want good things for me?
2. What are my personal goals, and does this comment strengthen me?
3. Does this comment strengthen my work?
4. Does this comment help me learn and grow?

1. Does this person really want good things for me?

I have an extended family member who has nothing but criticism for me. He's older and he's never been an entrepreneur, author, educator or feature film director. Those are my areas of expertise. However, this person just wants to make me "wrong." Wait a minute! This is a family member, but his goal is "to be right" and "to put the other person down." It's sad really.

When you consider whether criticism has merit, consider the source. If someone is in your target market, that criticism may be useful. However, if someone is merely guessing and has never entered the field you're working in, assess whether to dismiss such criticism.

Talking to my negative extended family member would be *where good ideas go to die*. So I often avoid this person. I have a circle of friends and colleagues who are supportive and still provide me with the constructive feedback that may be hard to hear, but their intention is good things for me. I can trust them.

2. What are my personal goals and does this comment strengthen me?

What are your real goals? Do you want to be famous? Do you want to do good artistic work? Do you want to make lots of money? Do you deeply long to express your creativity?

All of the above have different elements attached to them.

It's important for you to be honest with yourself. What do you really want?

The truth is that I want to serve my readers, audiences, graduate students and clients. So I'm willing to hear tough feedback and learn about areas to improve for my projects. For each book I write, I have at least two editors. They can be really tough and they push me to write in better ways. That's what I really want. I do not want to be coddled.

So even if my editors might occasionally clothe a comment with sarcasm, I still know that their comments actually strengthen me. After writing 28 books, I'm a better writer today.

Also, pause and get access to your own intuition. Often, some people are so quick to judge and say, "That won't work." How do they know? And imagine this: If your intuition is correct and you follow your heart—and you succeed—what will they say? They'll merely shrug and mildly reply, "Oh, I guess I was wrong on that one." Do *not* leave your fate to someone else. ***Answer your own heart's call.***

To take this conversation to the next step, view my 7 min. video "How to Believe in Yourself When Others Don't" (on YouTube.com).

3. Does this comment strengthen my work?

This is where the real work takes place. A tough comment like "I think that totally fails to engage your target market" may be the best reality check that you need. For example, with a video related to my science fiction franchise *TimePulse*, my team hit a wall. We needed a paragraph to bridge two sections of the video. I had four people tell me that the draft of the paragraph missed the mark. Okay. Back to the drawing board. Eventually, we came up with a solution. With a new approach, we found an appropriate quote to bridge the sections. [See our 1 minute video of science fiction and action, *TimePulse,* on YouTube.com— Search for "TimePulse Tom Marcoux."]

4. Does this comment help me learn and grow?

My team members know that I can calmly listen to any comment that points out flaws in a draft of a project. I'll often ask follow-up questions. Why? I'm focused on learning and growing as an artist in the various fields I participate in: speaking, writing, filmmaking and art direction of graphic novels.

My point is that a truly creative person must develop a "thick skin" and also run criticism through a filter. Some critical comments have nothing to do with your goals. Let them flow past like leaves on a stream of water.

Other comments, given as support and which strengthen your work, may raise your work to world-class level. It's an adventure that is actually worth the pain and effort. It's a road that includes surprising, happy moments.

What are your real goals with your project/career? Who has the real feedback that can help you improve your project? Reflect deeply: Who do you want to support your work but the person simply does *not* support your work? Where else can you look for real support and guidance (a coach*, an instructor, someone else)?

---

* Tom Marcoux, Executive Coach – Spoken Word Strategist works with clients . . . tomsupercoach@gmail.com

DISCOVER THE POWER OF
"LEAD SO I FOLLOW, SPEAK SO I BELIEVE"

How often do you hear someone say something positive about a leader or a manager? Not often. Why? We have some subconscious expectations of what good leaders do. I coined this phrase: "Lead So I Follow, Speak So I Believe."

I have led teams since I was nine years old, directing my first film. I've focused on being a good leader for decades. As a CEO, I currently lead teams in the United Kingdom, India and the USA. I've worked with mentors to develop my leadership skills. Further, as an Executive Coach and Spoken Word Strategist, I guide and support leaders to increase their impact and influence.

"Lead So I Follow, Speak So I Believe" is the experience that I want my team members to have. "I" stands for my team member.

Good leadership is *not* about the leader's ego. It's about making it possible to get things done and to have team members be clear about "the mission and the mighty." By

61

this I mean, the leader shows *how the team member can excel* and "be mighty."

"Speak So I Believe" is about the team member believing that she *can* succeed. It's also about people believing that the project is worthwhile. No one ever got excited by a leader saying, "Come join us. We're doing something mediocre."

"Speak So I Believe" is about **the team member believing that "I can trust *this* leader."**

N – nurture dialogue
O – own your positive language (drop "Loser Language")
W – wonder

1. Nurture dialogue

"Whoever does the most talking has the most fun." – Ruth Reed

Good leadership is not focused on "slick talk." Many of us can see through that. It comes from empowering questions.

When you, as the leader, ask empowering questions, then the team member will have the fun of talking. More than that, you as the leader, will learn a lot about what is going on in your team and in the individual team members.

Use "Headlines" and "Taglines" ("Taglines get the dialogue going.")

An effective leader gives the *headline* like: "I'm now going to talk about three possible solutions to the XY situation."

Then, the leader shows that she or he is open to input by using a *tagline* like this: "After I discuss the three possible solutions, I'm going to open this up. I want to hear your ideas, thoughts and feelings."

How do you eliminate miscommunication and confusion?

When you express a **headline**, the listener **understands your point up front.**

When you use a **tagline**, the listener *feels comfortable and primed to offer useful ideas for the discussion.*

Start in a Positive Manner

As the leader, you set the tone. Do *not* let loudmouth team members start every meeting as a "complaining fest."

Instead, start a meeting with this question: "Who has an appreciation to mention about someone or something that's working?"

2. Own your positive language (drop "Loser Language")

Leaders had better get this fact clear in mind: You're *the leader* not a casual friend.

You know what we do as friends: If a friend wants to complain, we go along. Sure, as a friend, you might be helpful in letting the other person vent.

On the other hand, as the leader, you do NOT let "victim language" or "Loser Language" escape your lips. You do *not* go along with a team member who just complains.

Sure, it may be tough to adapt to a new change required by a shift in the marketplace. But *as the leader*, you come in with comments and questions like:

- Okay. Dealing with this change is going to take effort. *We're good at this.* We're good at adapting and *surpassing.*
- Who has some ideas in how we can do this better?
- What did we learn here? How can we use what we learned to streamline the process?

When Steve Jobs returned to Apple, he *canceled* a number of projects. Jobs said, "Focus is about saying, *No*. And the result of that focus is going to be some really great products where the total is much greater than the sum of the parts."

I invite you to **cancel** "victim talk" or the alliterative "Loser Language." Instead of saying, like a victim, "Oh. It's going to be hard. Oh, it's not fair that we have to change again"—**you take command and, as the great leader, you say**, "It takes effort AND we're good at this. How do we take this circumstance and come back stronger?"

3. Wonder

The great leader is always on top of the numbers (for example, the number of marketing phone calls made this week by the sales team). And the great leader is always *wondering* about: How do we streamline this? How do we solve the bottleneck problem and improve the system? How do we serve the client better and double our reorders?

The great leader is not required to always have an answer. Instead, it's about *having the right questions.*

Inside the leader asks herself or himself:

- How can I express my certainty that this team can handle the situation? How do I reassure team members?
- (If the team must face a tough real situation) How can I tell the truth about this up front and guide the team out of pain and into positive action?
- How can I point out a specific accomplishment Max made and let him know I really appreciate it? (And this will get Max to keep doing the good

work. An old phrase is: What gets rewarded, get repeated.)

Outside, the leader asks team members:

- What needs to improve here?
- What's working?
- What do we need to enhance?
- What makes this project excellent?
- What do the stakeholders (clients, board of directors, others) really want here?

* * *

Now it's your turn.

Focus on this phrase: **"Lead So I Can Follow, Speak So I Believe."**

The great leader sets the tone, points to the goals, and leads the team from the front.

I remember directing a student film many years ago. We were running out of time on the location. The camera operator was ill and sitting down. I grabbed the tripod and said, "Everyone, we're going this way." And the team followed me.

Think of a situation in which you need to provide leadership. What would help people believe in you and trust you? How can you use a "headline" to clue the people into your point? How can you use a "tagline" to show that you want to hear the team's ideas, thoughts and feelings?

_____

_____

_____

_____

_____

USE SECRETS SO YOU BREAK THROUGH
AND LIVE YOUR DREAM!

"Sure, I'd live my dream—if I just knew how to get started," my friend Sam said.

"I can help you with that. First, I'll share 3 Principles that empower you to make massive progress," I replied.

We'll use the W.I.N. process:

W- work it through

I – identify "if in doubt, leave it out"

N – nurture flexibility

1. Work it through

Avoid a lot of wasted time and even pain when you *think it through* or take a pen and write details down to "work it through." I learned how helpful this process is—decades ago. I have directed films since I was nine years old. I've learned to *plan ahead and anticipate what can go wrong*—because things go wrong.

For example, I was directing a feature film some years

ago. We were set up on the tarmac where planes take off. (This was before the 911 Tragedies.)

The airport promised me three hours. After *only one hour*, an official arrived and said, "Pack up. You need to leave."

This would have been a disaster *if* I hadn't planned for it.

The night before, I worked it through in my mind and on paper. It was possible that I wouldn't get the whole time on the take-off tarmac. So I drew my storyboards and devised a prioritized shot list.

So I filmed all the essential moments first.

Then, when confronted by trouble of the unfair shortening of location time, I told my co-producer, "Have the equipment and the extras move slowly and start the 'leaving process.' I'll keep filming."

It came down to me (as a lead actor) and the cameraman getting some final shots.

All the while, my team is saying, "Yes—we're leaving. We're leaving."

My point is *work it through.* Figure out what can go wrong and how you can be sure to be okay or even triumph still.

Gail Anne Hurd, executive producer of the TV Show *The Walking Dead* and producer of *Terminator* (the first film of the series) said, "I always have a Plan B and Plan C."

As an Executive Coach, I work with clients so they think through their plans, then save time and resources as they achieve big accomplishments.

2. Identify "if in doubt, leave it out"

When I say "identify if in doubt, leave it out," I talking about zeroing in on things that I may have a doubt about. **If I have a doubt, it might be my intuition giving me a warning.**

For example, I recently spoke to an audience about the importance of listening to your intuition.

I said, "If your intuition says, 'Don't get on the elevator with that person.' Listen! Stay off that elevator. Some people tell themselves, 'Oh, I'm just being silly. I don't want to look foolish and not get on the elevator.' Do you know what we call people who don't listen to their intuition? Dead."

The audience laughed.

It was probably my timing with the word "dead."

Still, I'm making an important point: *If in doubt, leave it out.*

In other words, if something feels wrong—do NOT go through with it.

Let's make this clear. Confidence is *not* comfort. Even when you're on the right path, you'll likely feel a bit nervous.

That's not what we're talking about.

We're focusing on those *"something's not right"* feelings.

Listen to those feelings.

Many people get into messes and later say, "I knew I should not do that! But I did it anyway. What a bad mistake!"

Avoid wasting your time and resources. Remember: *If in doubt, leave it out.*

3. Nurture flexibility

To really make a dream come true, it helps to learn to "share the burden."

Nothing is impossible for the [person] who doesn't have to do it himself. – A. H. Weiler

Be flexible in your thinking. Look at situations from the other person's point of view.

For example, I'm still excited about the completion of my graphic novel *Crystal Pegasus*.

You notice that there are 10 names on the front cover.

We had a team of illustrators, colorists and an associate art director. And they are all credited on the front cover.

That may be unusual. Still, people have more fun and devote more productive energy when they know that they will be recognized for their contribution—on the front cover!

Answer these questions for yourself:

- How can you be flexible in your approach to your project?
- How can you get more help?
- How can you do something to truly recognize each person's contribution to the project?

To unlock more opportunities to fulfill your Dream, remember to W.I.N.

W- work it through
I – identify "if in doubt, leave it out"
N – nurture flexibility

Truly enjoy your life; step forward and fulfill your Dream.

How can you devote more time to think through a situation? Who can you turn to and "talk out loud" about your thoughts, feelings and intuition about the situation? Do you feel any "something is not right" feelings?

Is it time to drop the project and choose a replacement? And how can you be flexible about the process?

_____

_____

_____

_____

_____

_____

_____

_____

SECRETS TO ENHANCE YOUR SUCCESS AND HAPPINESS—FROM DIRECTING ON A MOVIE SET!

When I have directed feature films, I told key crew people **2 Key Principles**. These principles can also help you increase your prosperity, enhance your health and boost your happiness.

The principles are:

1) Protect the Talent

2) Guard Momentum

1. Protect the Talent

On a movie set, *the talent* are the actors. I have heard crew members grumble about how actors can rest in their trailer most of the day. The stand-ins are called to take the position of the lead actors as the director of photography has crew members adjust the lights.

Here's the point. The talent/actors need to be *well-rested* to perform at their best in the crucial moments when the movie camera is capturing the action.

You, in your own life, are the Talent. You need to be well-rested before you arrive at a meeting, give a speech or perform in a job interview. No one can take your place.

Here's the truth: No one cares as much as you do about what happens in your own life. And, no one else can feel *your intuition's call* that moves you toward your destiny.

So your must Protect the Talent: protect your own personal energy.

On the other hand, my father has sent a mudslide of opinions at me my whole life. But *he has never* jumped into the adventures I have had: directing and acting in feature films, guest-lecturing at Stanford University, lead singing (and song composing) for a band, and more. My father only knew about his career as a letter carrier ("mailman"). His opinions were like mud that could cause me to slip! **So I learned to move forward and listen to My Own Heart.**

I invite you to Protect the Talent—that is, *protect your own heart.* Listen to your intuition. How do you know that it's your intuition? Here's the distinction:

Your Intuition calls you: to expand, experiment, try something new, get coaching, take an appropriate risk.

Your Fear calls you: to contract, hide, avoid an appropriate risk.

Protect the Talent. Protect yourself from disempowering opinions. By the way, **do get some advice**—*from someone who has accomplished what you want to do!*

As an Executive Coach, I have a distinction: I am a *CEO who helps Leaders Maximize their Influence and Impact.* I lead teams in the United Kingdom, India and the United States of America. So I'm not talking from theory. I'm talking from my experience in leading teams since I was nine years old, making my first film. For example, I directed a feature film that went to the Cannes Film market and gained international distribution. I deeply know about leadership.

See my 1.8 min. video "'Lead So I Follow, Speak So I Believe' by Tom Marcoux" at YouTube.com

Guard Momentum

I'll say this in few words: **Guard Momentum or Miss Out on Much in Life.**

I'm sometimes stunned at how friends and family can actually sabotage your momentum. They may be afraid for you, but they do not realize that your pain and effort are *worth it to you!*

What's going on here? Your friends or family members do not feel your destiny. They are not comforted by your personal vision. Bluntly speaking, they may not be a similar type of person as you. Some people merely seek comfort.

As an Executive Coach – Spoken Word Strategist, I explain to clients: **"Confidence is NOT comfort."** If you're feeling some nervousness, that's good. Why? Because you care! As a trained actor and director, I know this: If the actor feels no nervousness before performing tonight's play then he or she does NOT care. Hence, a lousy performance.

Nervousness simply means that you care. What you do is *take that energy and convert into your "get ready energy."* This "get ready energy" empowers you for preparation before an event.

Along this line, **Confidence arises from rehearsal.** Through rehearsal, you start to feel it "in your bones" that you *know* that you know!

Here's where "Guard Momentum" comes in:

Once you have momentum going, the universe bends in your favor. Things get done more easily! It's true.

I remember when the name for my blog YourBodySoulandProsperity.com came together. **There was no agony. We had momentum that day.** The ideas flowed, and within 8 minutes, I was certain and I paid for the Domain Name.

Also . . .

Guard Momentum from your own self-sabotaging habits. Some of us start writing well and then say, "Oh, that's going well; I'll get a cup of coffee." No! Keep with it. Stay on a roll.

On a movie set, the director sets the pace. Every time I direct the crew to move the camera, it's called a "setup." That is, you set up the camera on the tripod or crane. To keep up momentum, I'll design my day of filming so we can quickly film different scenes. For example, I filmed in one direction on a street. Then I had the camera face the other direction, and I filmed another scene (for another section of the film). I kept up a fast pace, and we did many setups per day.

Clint Eastwood, as a director, is known for doing a lot of setups in a day. Clint is also know for only filming a couple of takes. His actors (both male and female) know to bring their "A-game" to the *first take.* It may be the only take they get! All of Clint's films come in under schedule and under budget. And the actors are happier. **Clint guards momentum.**

When you want more success in your life . . .

1) Protect the Talent

Get enough sleep, exercise, nutritious food and appropriate breaks *for yourself.*

2) Guard Momentum

Protect yourself from your own self-sabotaging behaviors to hesitate or procrastinate; make daily progress; do *not* let people talk you out of getting things done.

Some time ago, I was writing book after book. I had a couple of friends who tried to talk me out of writing at such a speedy pace. I'd have three editors simultaneously working on different sections of a business book I was writing. Here's the point: None of the naysayers had ever written a book. [Remember, I said, *"Get advice from someone who has **accomplished** what you want to do!"*]

By the way, the naysayers were often bellyaching about their lives.

I was having fun in writing the books (even with the hard work involved).

So I wrote 28 books. And two of those friends *moved themselves* out of my life. What a relief!

When you *Protect the Talent* and *Guard Momentum*, you have the opportunity to live in a joyful way.

When you say you fear death, you are really saying that you fear that you have not lived your true life." – Dr. David Viscott

"People living deeply have no fear of death." – Anais Nin

Some might think the above statements are extreme.

Still, we can see that living with courage and taking appropriate risks form a joy-filled journey.

How will you make today count?

How can you take better care of yourself? How can you get breaks during the long haul of a project? . . . How can you guard your momentum? What social events might you

need to bow out of to—guard your momentum?

DON'T LET OTHERS SHUT DOWN YOUR DREAM!—PROTECT YOUR DREAM

Protect your Dream. Feed your soul and hold a "shield" to block others' distractions and comparisons. We'll use the A.I.M. process:

A – align with your "heart energy"
I – intensify coaching
M – measure through meaning

1. Align with your "heart energy"

My father gave me a backhanded gift: His denial of approval. When confronted with that withholding of approval these many years, *I learned to listen to my own heart and my intuition.*

When I say "align with your heart energy," I'm talking about focusing on *what makes your heart sing.*

I've learned from directing feature films and writing 28 books that you cannot count on results. Find something that you want to put your heartfelt efforts into. You do your best, and the results turn out the way they turn out.

Don't let other people tell you what's important. For example, feature film director Norman Jewison suffered a box office bomb called *The Art of Love*. No one remembers that film today. But we still remember Norman's films: *In the Heat of the Night*; *Fiddler on the Roof*; and *Moonstruck* (starring Cher and Nicholas Cage).

Norman put his heart into his films. *That's what counts.* Sometimes lots of people respond favorably. Sometimes, they don't.

Keep moving forward.

By the way, view my 7 minute video: "How to Believe in Yourself When Others Don't" at YouTube.com.

2. Intensify coaching

Beware of letting random opinions shut you down emotionally. My father dumped opinions on me. Still, he had *no clue* about directing films, singing in a band, writing songs, writing books, and creating graphic novels. Unlike my journey, he had *no* experience in leading teams in the United Kingdom, India and the United States of America.

What my father knows about is being a letter carrier (now a retired mailman). After 30 years of service in the US Postal Service, he has one comment: "Use FedEx."

Whenever, I wanted to do something unusual, I got coaching from *someone who knows the field I would next explore.*

When I first entered the speaking industry, I hired a coach and, with guidance, moved forward fast. *(As an Executive Coach – Spoken Word Strategist, that's what I do today. One client, Brad Carlson said, "Tom Marcoux coached me to get more done in 10 days than other coaches in 2 years."*

I've hired more than 8 editors. I've learned from each one. Along the way, I've written 28 books and countless articles (over 2 million words). Some people like my writing and others don't. The naysayers do not stop me. I know a particular writer who looked with disdain at my writing. While he was criticizing, I wrote 27 books and he wrote none. He stepped out of my life. What a relief!

My friend, protect your dream. Do *not* let naysayers shut down your dream.

Don't let uninformed opinions shut down your dream. Get suitable and empowering coaching.

3. Measure through meaning

By "measure through meaning," I'm referring to an empowering practice of choosing significant ways to measure the value of what you're doing.

For example, as an Executive Coach, I coached a particular client in developing a blog that started from zero to blog-visitors from 141 countries.

I noticed that my client would get stuck in worrying about "how many people are following today" and "ooh! I lost a follower of my blog!"

To focus on meaning, I then asked her:
- Are you writing from your heart?
- Are you glad that people are responding to your postings?
- Do you feel that your blog is worth it if 20 people are helped? 10? One person?

My point is: **You pick what is meaningful.**

Be aware of how easy it is to become addicted to "the numbers." Some people "live" for just seeing whether the number of blog visitors has risen today.

Other people are living well <u>while they are writing</u> the current blog post.

Choose to focus on what really means a lot to you.

Find something healthy and uplifting *and meaningful* to focus on.

* * *

Realize that there is a big difference between *supportive coaching*, and some people who act like crabs. The phrase "crab mentality" refers to a behavior of crabs in a boiling pot. One crab tries to escape and *the other crabs pull down* that smart, trying to get away crab. It's like the other crabs have a plan, "We'll make you die, too. We will *not* work together so that we can all escape."

Realize that your Dream is your escape from the boiling pot of a frustrated, empty life.

Identify the crabs in your life, and guard your personal energy. Eliminate time around crabs. If a crab is a family member, then, perhaps, you can greatly reduce your exposure to this person.

Do not let others shut down your dream.

Instead, **nurture yourself.**

The world will be better with your positive creativity in it.

Who do you know who "acts like a crab" toward you? In other words, who around you is "pulling you down" and ultimately hurting you? How can you reduce time around that person? How can you nurture yourself more so you can unleash your positive creativity?

_____

_____

_____

_____

_____

_____

_____

_____

USE THE REAL SECRET SO YOU BECOME STRONGER AND LEAP TO HIGHER LEVELS OF SUCCESS

Tired of the usual "here's how to be successful" talk? Here's the truth: You want success?—take massive strategic action and *handle rejection well*—and put yourself in plenty of situations where rejection can occur. The most successful people I have interviewed get rejected every month. Why? Because they're always stretching, growing, trying new things and contacting new people. And they're inviting people to support their projects or purchase their products. Or they're pulling people together to make things happen. **Top professionals handle rejection well.** Here is a process that can help you do well in the face of rejection: We'll use the C.A.N. process:

C – cancel "rejection" in favor of "we did not have match"
A – appreciate
N – notice

1. Cancel "rejection" in favor of "we did not have match"

If you feel bad, you're probably thinking some disempowering thought like "they rejected me." Now, imagine a "cancel" button. Then visualize pressing the button and simultaneously say aloud, "We did not have a match." In this way, you are taking action to reframe your view of the situation. To "reframe" is to shift your interpretation. Instead of the disempowering idea "they rejected me" you can "press the cancel button" and replace the first idea with something better: "We did not have a match."

Unfortunately, "they rejected me" carries the baggage of "there must be something wrong with me." Instead, when you use the neutral "we did not have a match" you avoid throwing a negative judgment upon yourself. Instead, you're allowing the idea that something neutral happened: There was no match.

Recently, a friend and I discussed "rejection." Suddenly, I had a thought: "You can't reject me (that is, reject my essence). I'm a spiritual being. But you certainly can disagree." When I say "disagree," I mean that someone can disagree with how I made something (a book, for example). In essence, they "disagree" about how useful the book is. I've learned that when you say something from your heart, some people will agree, some will disagree and others will ignore it. That's all okay (even if it's tough to take sometimes). I remind myself that it is okay that "we did not have a match."

2. Appreciate

When you do something original, some people will NOT like it. Great! You've done something. If you did nothing, there would be nothing to disagree with [or "reject."]

If you didn't show up for the job interview, there would be no possibility for a positive response or a negative response. **So appreciate your courage and your efforts.** You are one step closer to a positive outcome.

One time when I felt the sting of a negative review, I decided that there must be some way I could turn around my feelings. That's when I devised something new: a **"Celebrate Someone Disagrees" Ritual.** In essence, I reward myself for having the courage to take a risk and "put my voice out there." My sweetheart listens to me as I write my books so I'll take her out to have a "Celebrate Someone Disagrees" Ritual. We may go to See's Candies—she usually wants to celebrate with chocolate. And we're likely to go to a bookstore, since I like to celebrate by getting a book. We're celebrating courage and taking action.

As an Executive Coach, I help clients use exercises and patterns to become stronger and take massive strategic action. When you take control of your patterns of thinking, you can bounce back faster and get more done!

3. Notice

Notice that it takes just a simple shift of thinking to go from sad and feeling rejected to a new pattern of thinking: "I'm okay. I'm proud of myself for putting my work out in the world."

Also, notice that people seem to be complaining a lot recently. Certainly, I've seen some really mean comments on YouTube.com. Along these lines . . . recently, I read how Barbara Walters held it together while being criticized early in her career. She received a note from John Wayne that read: "Don't let the bastards get you down." Well, that was concise.

My point is that the people I know who enjoy fulfillment are the ones who are creating artwork and getting things done. They refuse to allow critical comments to slow them down. Let the critics amuse themselves with criticizing. But let you and I find fulfillment in expressing ourselves and learning as we go.

I remember Steven Spielberg said, "I don't have to prove anything to anyone. And I don't have to prove anything to myself. I just need to stay interested." As an Executive Coach, I help clients connect with their "Big Energy," which is connected to their heart. Certainly, Steven Spielberg is connected with his own Big Energy. With such Big Energy, *you can face the tough situations* and the bumpy parts of your journey. You will not stop. You may slow a bit, but *you have the personal power to persist and triumph.*

So I invite you to celebrate each rejection—because you are one of the few courageous people who goes out and expresses yourself and gets things done. Remember to treat yourself to a "Celebrate Someone Disagrees" Ritual (reward).

This morning I awoke with this thought: "Blessed are the Dreamers for they're the ones who show the way."

I might amend the phrase to *"Dreamers Who Are Doing."* If you're doing something, you'll likely face criticism. That's okay. Celebrate your courage. Celebrate learning new things. Yes—Celebrate Someone Disagrees.

And keep moving forward.

How can you celebrate your courage? What will you designate as your "Celebrate Someone Disagrees" Ritual? How can you be especially kind to yourself when you endure a rejection? How can you be good to yourself and

then go into positive action?

_____

_____

_____

_____

_____

_____

_____

_____

MAKE YOUR LIFE TAKE FLIGHT— STOP WAITING!

What stands between you and true success and fulfillment? Waiting. For what? Some of us wait for that one dream that will make all the hard work worth it. **Stop waiting! Why? You'll find better projects, methods and reasons for your efforts** *along* **the road of your life.** You cannot see nor even imagine what possibilities are coming. Why? When you rise to a new peak, you can see new things —like other new peaks (which could be opportunities).

"Courage is not the absence of fear but rather the judgment that something is more important than fear." – Meg Cabot

What could be more important than fear? *Your personal reason to do something.*

Some people say that want financial abundance. Why do they want more cash? As an Executive Coach, I've asked clients why they want more money. Here are some of their answers:

- no worries about paying bills
- the freedom to choose my own creative projects
- the chance to enjoy travel, vacations, a new home and more
- the ability to protect my loved ones from suffering after I've passed away.

Whatever your personal reason is at this moment . . . **get into action.** Try new things. Take an appropriate risk. Listen to your intuition.

Here's a personal example. Yesterday, a friend asked me, "Tell me about something you're happy about." I replied, "I'm happy that my fantasy graphic novel *Crystal Pegasus* is up on Amazon.com."

"Crystal Pegasus" began as a little story told by a day camp counselor to the little kids in his charge. The day camp counselor was *the lead character in a screenplay I wrote several years ago* that served as my introduction to the film industry.

Then look what happened:

1) When I was directing a feature film based on a different screenplay, *the screenplay featuring Crystal Pegasus* impressed the then-California Motion Picture Commissioner. He helped me gain the San Luis Obispo airport and an American Eagle airplane for me to use *for free* in the production of my feature film.

2) Later, I filmed some portions of the screenplay, including a scene in which I, as the lead character, told the story, "Crystal Pegasus" to summer day camp kids.

3) I later finished an audio novel based on the screenplay.

4) Then I converted that story "Crystal Pegasus" into a form that could be a 15 page little book for kids.

Finally, with a team of 10 people, that little story grew into *Crystal Pegasus*, the 90 page graphic novel for children and others.

I had no idea that my screenplay would flow through transformations over the years, and a portion of it would later yield a graphic novel *Crystal Pegasus*.

I've shared this above example to illustrate that **taking action can lead in surprising and positive, new directions.**

So I invite you to **stop waiting!**

As an Executive Coach, I provide the support that my clients need to see the whole picture, *create* a plan, *rehearse* for important events and *take consistent action.*

How can your adventure begin if you take no action?

Try something new and see what develops.

Tell yourself the truth: What are you procrastinating on? What are you waiting for? What can you do *today* to make some progress toward fulfilling your dreams?

_____

_____

_____

_____

USE THE REAL SECRET OF THREE-DIMENSIONAL SUCCESS

Imagine the man who arrived at success just in time to lose his marriage. Or the woman who took care of everyone but herself and died young. That's successful? I'm introducing "Success in 3 Dimensions."

Success in 3 Dimensions
- you feel great
- you're doing well in creating abundance
- your health is terrific.

Having all three dimensions is essential to enjoying your successful life. When I say, "Doing well in creating abundance" I'm referring to a number of elements. Many of us truly want to enjoy what we do for a living. Further, we want to be well-compensated. And the idea of "abundance" is useful. Abundance is about having a surplus—more than enough. If you have barely enough to pay rent and eat, that's *not* fun!

Many of us want cash to take a vacation, celebrate a loved one's birthday and more.

The question is: How can I have all three dimensions: feel great, create abundance and enjoy terrific health?

Here's the Real Secret of 3-Dimensional Success: It consists of three parts.

- "Life is about success, not perfection." – Alan Weiss
- "It does not matter how slow you go as long as you do not stop." – Confucius
- "Do something. It's Better than Zero." – Tom Marcoux

As an Executive Coach, I help my client devise an action plan that supports a great life of feeling great, doing well in creating abundance and enhancing one's health.

1) "Life is about success, not perfection." – Alan Weiss

The problem with perfectionism is that it may shut down a person so he or she is afraid to do something because of fear about not excelling at it the first time.

If life is about success, then you can pay close attention and identify the vital elements of having a successful business, a successful relationship and good health. As human beings, we're unlikely to do everything "perfectly," but we can focus on the *Most Important Things*.

For example, one of my clients walks 30 minutes a day and during that time talks with her boyfriend. Sure, perfection would include her doing vigorous weight training and running for two hours each day—but that does not match her lifestyle. So her body is not "perfect" in her *own* mind. But she does have a good romantic relationship; she's doing well at work and she gets appropriate sleep. These are *important elements* of a successful life.

Another way to view "success not perfection" is to declare: **Life is about taking effective action and making consistent progress.**

Now it's your turn.

Where are you allowing perfectionism to slow you down? Are you spending your energy on "small things" and are you neglecting the most important things that can improve your life?

2) "It does not matter how slow you go as long as you do not stop." – Confucius

Many of us have heard of the overnight success that took ten years.

My dad told me, "It takes fifteen years to be an overnight success," and it took me seventeen and a half years.
– Adrien Brody

The journey is important. Recently, I was teaching people how to go from zero connections to blog visitors from 141 countries. I realized that I had trained my whole life to teach that session and those people on that day.

Earlier in my business career, I worked for corporations doing work that had nothing to do with my best talents. Then, a decade later, I applied what I had learned to teaching graduate students at Stanford University.

All the experiences add up to make me more valuable to the marketplace today!

Now it's your turn.

How might you apply what you've learned over the years

to making your life better and better?

3) "Do something. It's Better than Zero." – Tom Marcoux

Sometimes, the thing to do is to study the situation or get more information. Sometimes the thing to do is to take a break! When you return, you'll have a fresh perspective. For example, a client presented me with her notes for a blog article. At first, I was baffled. The notes were convoluted. I took a break and returned and BAM! I could see the hidden thread that could run through the blog article.

My main point about "Do something. It's Better than Zero" is: *Take a step forward each day; they add up* . . . Two hundred words a day leads to a 52,000 word book (for example).

Laura Hillenbrand, the author of the bestselling books *Seabiscuit* and *Unbroken* endures Chronic Fatigue Syndrome. The article "The Unbreakable Laura Hillenbrand" notes: "Even the physical act of writing can occasionally stymie [Laura], as the room spins and her brain swims to find words in a cognitive haze. There have been weeks and months—indeed, sometimes years—when the mere effort to lift her hands and write has been all that she can muster."

Still, Laura takes a few steps forward each day. Let's notice that it all adds up: *Seabiscuit* has 399 pages and *Unbroken* includes 528 pages.

By the way, Laura's success is unusual. She does no talk shows and no in-person appearances promoting her books. And still, her books are bestsellers.

Now it's your turn.

What can you do today that is "better than zero"? How can you take some steps forward each day?

As an Executive Coach, I help my client express what's in

his or her heart, create a powerful plan, and take action consistently.

Remember, the people who truly enjoy life are making progress in all 3 Dimensions of Success:

- they feel great
- they're doing well in creating abundance
- their health is terrific.

Remember "Life is about success, not perfection."

My added comment is: **Boldness makes progress. Precision makes sustainability.** By this I mean, you need to take a courageous step forward. You can refine your work as you go along so your work has lasting power.

Take some steps forward today.

How are you approaching things in a "perfectionist way"? How can you set up your own standards so you're focused on success and NOT "perfection?" How have you held yourself back by deeming the situation or yourself as "not good enough"? Will you put yourself into positive action and make some form of progress today?

_____

_____

_____

_____

_____

LOVE YOURSELF TO
FINANCIAL ABUNDANCE

I recently saw four of my friends have money troubles and I had a surprising thought: "If they loved themselves more, they would have been in better shape." Then, my thoughts crystallized when I saw my cat walk into the room where I was typing on a desktop computer.

I realized that my cat naturally does three things–and these can apply toward increasing one's financial abundance.

1. Be yourself

My cat, Magic, simply expresses himself as a cat. He doesn't try to bark or chase cars.

Now, how does this apply to increasing our financial abundance? I'll give you an example. Some years ago, I sat in a room of 23 attorneys who did not want to be attorneys. They had the law degree but then discovered that they did not find the day-to-day work appealing. These were *not* happy, successful attorneys!

My point is that we are less likely to excel at what we do not like. And often what we do not like relates to where our skills and native ability is lacking.

Instead, focus on your areas of great interest.

Secondly, don't compete—be yourself and create. To create more financial abundance, it's often better to **create your own category** instead of trying to jump into a category that already has intense, existing competition.

For example, there is no one just like Whoopi Goldberg. She's an African American woman named after a cushion and a Jewish person. How's that?

We're here for a reason. I believe a bit of the reason is to throw little torches out to lead people through the dark.
— Whoopi Goldberg

2. Be where you can get what you want

I frequently encounter my cat in the kitchen. Why? That's where the food is. It's simple. He wants a treat, and he's next to the refrigerator.

Now, it's your turn:

What do you want? And where is it?

For example, let's say you want to raise money for making a feature film. Where are the film investors? Some years ago, I attended a meeting in Palo Alto, California. In the meeting were film investors. If a filmmaker wanted to have a chance to get funded by these particular investors, he or she needed to be in that room at that time.

For some forms of business, you need to go where the fans are. At one point, there was a TV show entitled *Heroes of Cosplay*, which featured people who travel to many comic book conventions. That's where the fans are.

3. Ask for what you want

I've just scratched under my cat's chin for the seventh time in a row. I'm not a cat owner; I am cat staff.

Magic speaks up and *asks for what he wants:* Attention and specifically to be scratched under his chin. When I scratch him behind the ears, he actually *lifts his chin* for me to scratch exactly where he wants.

How does this apply to increasing your financial abundance? In the following ways:

You need to . . .

- ask for the sale
- ask for someone to take a moment and listen to you
- ask for help
- ask for support
- ask for new ideas
- ask for referrals for your business

A Special Note about *Love Yourself to Financial Abundance:*

I'm emphasizing "love yourself" because, for many of us, to increase our income we're going to need to do new things and sometimes put in extreme efforts. We need to *take great care of ourselves* because we need extra energy to do extraordinary things.

When you love a child, you make sure the little one brushes his or her teeth. The child will likely give you resistance, but you'll brave it because the child's well-being is of primary importance. When you love yourself, you'll do the tough things to make sure that you *become the person you want to be, who attracts success and financial abundance.* [This is so important to me that I wrote a whole book on the topic: *Love Yourself to Financial Abundance and Spiritual Joy: How You Can Remove Blocks to Your Prosperity, Happiness and Inner Peace* – See a Free Chapter at Amazon.com]

For example, I started off as a shy, nine-year-old boy, terrified while playing the piano for seniors in a retirement home. *So I gained the coaching and training—and did hours of rehearsal—*to become a professional speaker and leader of companies. Why? *Because I wanted to get big things done.* I loved myself enough to invest in my training. I was also realistic in understanding that a lot of rehearsal would help develop new skills and new patterns of speaking and performing.

As an Executive Coach, I assure my clients about *the power of having someone support you as you stretch and grow.* **This is a fact I know**. I had three excellent high school instructors:

- One taught psychology—I earned a degree in psychology.
- One taught English literature—I wrote 28 books and screenplays—and directed feature films.
- One taught theology—I wrote a college online course in Comparative Religion that I have been teaching for over 13 years.

Some time ago, I posted a question to my 5,795 Facebook contacts—and I submit it to you now:

What positive thing would you do if you loved yourself enough or loved yourself more?

Write down your answer.

Make a plan.

And take action to expand your financial abundance.

In essence, *love yourself to financial abundance.*

What positive thing(s) would you do if you loved yourself enough or loved yourself more? . . . How might you take better care of yourself and do something to increase your financial abundance?

_____

_____

_____

_____

_____

_____

_____

_____

_____

HOW YOU CAN GET STRONG, OVERCOME PAIN AND MAKE YOUR LIFE BETTER!

Ever hit a wall of grief and pain? The road of healing includes guiding your thoughts to positive possibilities — even while giving yourself space to do some grieving. I'll share three questions that help you step forward in life.

When we really face it, we have two things: this present moment and the next moment. But many of us get stuck in either guilt/regrets of the past or worries of the future.

What brings us to this present moment? A question.

Some questions empower us. And others tear us down like: "Why does this always happen to me?" or "When will I stop being [clumsy, stupid . . . any other self-degrading remark]?"

Instead, an empowering question will turn the direction of your thoughts to what you can use to improve this moment and the next moment.

Here are 3 Power Questions my clients use:
- What did I learn?

- What did Higher Power want me to get from this?
- How can I move forward and carry the lesson for the better?

For those people who have a spiritual path, the second question gets them out of their own ego.

I have learned, as I was grieving the death of a close friend, that I could learn a number of lessons.

For example, after a close friend committed suicide, I supported another friend "Sam" by asking, "Do you need a suicide watch?" [A suicide watch is when friends take shifts so someone will be with a depressed person 24/7.] That took courage because I risked Sam's anger.

However, Sam said, "Thank you for being concerned. I am okay."

I invite you to use these three questions. Discover what next positive thing can be part of your life journey.

Here's another important detail. I have learned to be grateful for what I have—and what I enjoyed in the past.

As I step into a new day and I find that some things change, I'll say, "I'm in a new chapter of my life. I'm grateful for what happened in the previous chapter. And I'm fully present for this new chapter."

As an Executive Coach, I help my client develop skills, strength and stamina. During the process, the client will take new action and take new appropriate risks. And there are times when life throws in some hardship.

So if you're experiencing some hardship (perhaps, losing a friend or a job or a possession like a totaled car), see if you can grieve AND employ the *3 Power Questions:*
- What did I learn?
- What did Higher Power want me to get from this?
- How can I move forward and carry the lesson for

the better?

A good journey to you.

Take a look at something that causes you pain and/or grief. Now apply the *3 Power Questions:* a) What did I learn? b) What did Higher Power want me to get from this? and c) How can I move forward and carry the lesson for the better? (Write about this at length.)

_____

_____

_____

_____

_____

_____

_____

_____

_____

DON'T LET FEAR SHUT DOWN YOUR CREATIVITY!

One decision can improve your life. It's when you decide to become strong and handle fear. This means a lot to me because I've had to face fear numerous times. They were various firsts: first time directing a feature film, first time being the lead singer/song-writer of a band, first time writing a book, first time teaching MBA students at Stanford University and more. I had some fear each time, but I went forward.

It comes down to four essential questions:

1) What's your safety net?

When I write a book, I have two editors who push me to better writing. I get support and I offer it, too. A little while ago, I launched my Linkedin.com group "Executive Public Speaking and Communication Power!" Consider joining the group.

2) How can you step past fears about money?

A little while ago, I started writing my first musical. I scheduled the work to happen over three years. Why? I'm busy doing other things that are the sources of income. I do not set myself up to have to earn money with the musical. I have the freedom to experiment.

No matter how the musical turns out, I will grow and improve as a writer. It will not interfere with my income-generating work. But it will be a source of fun and creative joy!

So concerns about money will not shut down my creativity.

As an Executive Coach, I help clients make a plan that inspires them and that comforts them because we develop the contingency plans to handle the bumpy road of fulfilling one's real potential and real destiny.

3) How can you do it without needing others to say "yes"?

When it comes to the musical, I do not have to wait for a theatre troupe to say *yes*. I can hire singers and record a version of the songs in a recording studio. I can say *yes* to myself. Maybe one of the songs will work well separately from the musical.

4) How can you focus on "learning" instead of allowing the fear "it may not be great" to stop you?

Do not let yourself get stuck in having to make anything "great" the first time out. Realize that any art form requires a learning curve.

For example, I know a number of people who have enjoyed *Wicked*, the musical. Some consider it the biggest stage success of composer Stephen Schwartz's career. In October 2010, *Wicked* became the third musical in Broadway history to exceed $500 million in total gross income. And *Wicked* is Stephen's thirteenth musical. Yes, it's a big hit and it's number 13. He just keeps on getting better!

Don't expect yourself to do it "perfectly" the first time. We truly learn by doing.

When you focus on learning each time you go to the creative well, you always win. Sometimes, you may do a project that does not hit the marketplace at a suitable time. For example, when the film *The Princess Bride* was released, few people saw it at movie theaters. Only later, a core audience found the film when it was released on VHS tape. It became so popular that it's now available on Blu-ray, and a while ago, it had a special 25th Anniversary edition. What counts is that you keep exploring and taking appropriate risks. (Get more encouragement. See a free chapter of my book *Nothing Can Stop You This Year!* at Amazon.com).

This reminds me of the quote:

"Don't ask what the world needs. Ask what makes you come alive, and go do it. Because what the world needs is people who have come alive." – Howard Thurman

As an Executive Coach, I help my clients connect with what I call "Big Energy," which helps them focus, plan and take consistent action.

Keep learning, keep expressing your creativity and you'll find joy in doing the projects. And you'll come alive!

Think of a project. Now apply the *4 Questions*:

1) What's your safety net?
2) How can you step past fears about money?
3) How can you do it without needing others to say "yes"?
4) How can you focus on "learning" instead of allowing the fear "it may not be great" to stop you?

_____

_____

_____

_____

_____

_____

_____

_____

USE "ONE YES FOR INFINITE SUCCESS"

Have you ever thought of someone who could say *yes* and change your whole life? Imagine knowing how to get the "One YES" that improves your life. The insights in this article are especially helpful when you want breakthroughs in prosperity. We'll use the O.N.E. process:

O – open your thoughts
N – notice a category
E – energize your contacts

1. Open your thoughts

What would be your "One YES" that massively improves your life?

For some it would be "Yes, we'll publish your book."

Others would welcome:

- Yes, I'll marry you.
- Yes, I'll invest in your company.
- Yes, I'll join your team.

Have you noticed that some people refuse to even speculate about something great happening? Why? Perhaps, they're trying to avoid feeling disappointed.

The truth is life brings disappointment even if we try to hide and hold tiny expectations.

For many of us, it is *better* **to have a "glorious direction" to aim for.**

When I say, *Open Your Thoughts*, I invite you to ask this question: What would make that person who can give the "One YES" take special notice of me and my project?

It could be:

a) You sold 20,000 copies of your graphic novel.
b) A notable person endorses your book.
c) A doctor has certified that your meditation audio program helps her patients.

Big possibilities begin when we *open our thoughts* to new ideas. Have the courage to imagine who can change your life with a "Yes" response. Then start preparing so you can impress them and get their cooperation.

As an Executive Coach, I support my client to do something on a small scale to show what she or he can do. It's all about demonstrating your skills and vision. You create credibility. You build from there, and the process can go surprisingly fast. For example, my clients have said:

- "Tom Marcoux coached me in 10 days to get more done than other coaches in 2 years." – Brad Carlson, CEO of Mindstrong LLC

- "Using just one of Tom Marcoux's methods, I got more done in 2 weeks than in 6 months." – Jaclyn Freitas, M.A.

The process is: open your thoughts, set a plan and take action. Then you enjoy feeling proud of yourself as you create new and better results.

2. Notice a category

Thinking of only ONE person and trying to be perfect in one meeting to get their cooperation may feel overwhelming. If I concentrate on only ONE person who can change my life, then I might be terrified of making a mistake. Instead, I think of a **"category of people"** who could say *yes.*

You see, it's not one person. It's a whole bunch of people who share a trait or two.

For example, when I enter a negotiation, I think, "Let's see if they want to play." In this manner, I reduce my level of nervousness.

We can apply this principle, in a way, to identifying a *category of people* who could give you that one Big Yes.

3. Energize your contacts.

As an Executive Coach, I often help clients focus on what I call the **3 Magic Words of Networking:** *Help Them First.* Find a way to be supportive of what the other person is doing. Develop warm connections.

Second, let the right people know what your big goals are.

For example, my team is focused on our franchise titled *Jack AngelSword* (which includes graphic novels and feature films).

My ultimate goal is: *Jack AngelSword* serves millions of people so near the end of my life, I can sell my company (that includes other franchises) to . . . you guessed it: Disney.

Why? Because I want my franchise to continue to inspire and serve people beyond my lifespan.

You've probably heard of the theory of "Six Degrees of Separation" which holds that everyone is merely six steps away. So all you need is an introduction from one person to another.

I know that this can work in your favor. For example, *when I first began in the film industry,* I wrote a screenplay that one software engineer handed to another software engineer —to a real estate developer—and then to the California Motion Picture Commissioner.

When I needed it, the California Motion Picture Commissioner **arranged for San Luis Obispo airport and an American Eagle airplane (for free) for a feature film I was directing.**

So in essence, I'm saying:

Energize your contacts.

You can make big things happen with the right people on board.

(By the way, who do you know who would like to connect with me about *Jack AngelSword?* Just asking.)

Think about this deeply. Who can say "yes" to you and such a response would make a Big Difference in your life? Do you need a coach, consultant, investor, producer, employer, or client to say "yes" to you? How can you develop more positive relationships with contacts so you have more opportunities to connect with people who can say "yes" to you?

_____

_____

_____

_____

_____

_____

_____

_____

STOP GIVING YOUR POWER AWAY!

You want more and better in your life, right? Then STOP giving your power away.

"What do you mean giving my power away? I'm doing my job," my friend, Serena, said.

"I hear you. For many of us, it's *really subtle* in how we're losing time, energy and focus to the 'trivial many' when we would do better in focusing on the Vital Few," I replied.

We'll use the N.O.W. process:

N – nurture your wisdom

O – overcome a mood

W – wake up to a "disempowering fixation"

1. Nurture your wisdom

What is the wise thing to do in a situation? You'll often know the best course of action when you make space to *pause, reflect and respond.*

Some of us give our power away by saying "yes" too quickly.

Just today, a couple of PR people from publishers asked me to review some books by writing articles at one of my blogs. I immediately replied that I'd study their materials as soon as I could.

Still, I did *not* agree to reviewing the books too fast.

I'm really busy working with clients and leading teams in the United Kingdom, India and the United States of America.

I make good choices. How? I give myself **"thinkspace."** I give myself the space and time to think through–and then make a good choice.

Another way to nurture your wisdom is to get access to much of the best thinking and case histories as possible. I consult my own coaches and mentors, and I read up to 81 books each year.

As an Executive Coach, I know my clients rely on me to serve in a number of roles as coach, business consultant, brand strategist, speech coach, and mentor. I need to be at the top of my game to help them with their game.

Finally, *nurture your wisdom by removing certain distractions.* That is, take good care yourself: enough sleep, exercise, good nutrition and breaks to refresh yourself.

2. Overcome a mood

Many of us give away our power to a current mood we're in.

For example, I've written more than 2 million words (and 28 books). How? **I do NOT wait to be in the mood to write.** I sit down and start writing. For the first five minutes, I may feel that I'm writing garbage but I press on.

I develop patterns of high productivity, and I assist my clients to develop their own positive patterns.

"Inspiration usually comes during work, rather than before it." – *Madeleine L'Engle*

"A professional is someone who can do his best work when he doesn't feel like it." – *Alistair Cooke*

Do *not* let a disempowering mood take away your power. **Do something to shift your mood.**

During workshops, I teach audience members to use a power-move and power-phrase. For example, when I am tired, but still need to do some writing, I tap my fist on my thigh and say, **"I CAN do this!"**

By the time I ascend the stairs to the second floor of my home, I'm ready to get right to work.

Now it's your turn.

How can you shift from a disempowering mood? What music energizes you? Or if you feel high strung: What music calms you down and soothes you?

Would taking a brief walk help you clear your mind?

3. Wake up to a "disempowering fixation"

Sometimes as I help clients build a brand up from "zero," I see the client get fixated on something.

For example, some clients get stuck on doing perfect graphics for an ebook or CD cover.

I share with them this idea: "Making your first ebook is part of 'making the running shoes' **and** *'we need you to get running.'"*

For many clients with a new brand, they really need to *get out there and do the marketing and selling*—and *not* wait for "the perfect business card."

Unfortunately, because it's more fun or simply easier, a number of people get stuck in a "disempowering fixation." Waiting until one has the perfect business card can be a disempowering fixation.

For example, someone who owns a company might get stuck in what is called an "occupational hobby." Let's say Stephanie started as a graphic designer, but now she runs a company with six employees. It's better for her to concentrate on *getting new clients* instead of tinkering with Photoshop.

Do not let some fixation or even addiction take away your power.

Face reality and identify what is Most Important for you to do.

How do you discover what is most important? Often, it's something you dread doing.

My phrase is: **What you dread moves you ahead.**

For example, you may dread updating your resume. But what is *most important* for your career?—updating your resume.

What's the solution? Use the practice of **"Worst First."** That is, you do the *worst task* early when you're fresh. If you need to update your resume, work on it *early* in your day.

You have the choice to do better in life.

Pay close attention. *Where are you giving your power away?*

Remember the N.O.W. process:

N – nurture your wisdom

O – overcome a mood

W – wake up to a "disempowering fixation"

Doing better often is *not* about doing more, *it's about dropping what does NOT work.*

Nurture your power.

What are you giving your power to (a project, a habit and addiction) that is causing you trouble? Is there some person you're giving your power to? Are you wasting your time trying to please someone who does not know how to be pleased?

How can you take better care of yourself? How can you

reserve time and energy for that which supports your highest good?

_____

_____

_____

_____

_____

_____

_____

_____

HOW YOU CAN "SOURCE BY DIVINE LOVE"

Want a source to feel better and more hopeful? We'll use the S.E.E. process:

S – source daily by Divine Love

E – erase the ego

E – engage

1. Source daily by Divine Love

To source is to get something from a particular place. What place? I suggest a place outside of depending on others to hold you up.

Where do you get your energy from? If you only feel good when you accomplish something or when someone approves of you, you may find yourself in an "energy crisis."

Instead, consider *doing something each day to connect with your Divine Source.* For over a 13 years, I teach Comparative Religion on the college level (and I wrote the online course). And I've observed that a number of spiritual paths suggest that a person pray or meditate to connect with a Divine Source.

My clients report that they
- meditate for 10 minutes in the morning
- go for a walk at a park at lunchtime
- pray
- practice deep breathing

To "source daily by Divine Love" is to make a bit of time and space to turn your perspective to an *expansive level*. What is the alternative? Many of us find it easy to settle for the perspective of "clod of ailments" as George Bernard Shaw mentioned in this quote:

This is the true joy in life, the being used for a purpose recognized by yourself as a mighty one; the being a force of nature instead of a feverish, selfish little clod of ailments and grievances complaining that the world will not devote itself to making you happy. – George Bernard Shaw

To "source by Divine Love" is to hold that there IS Divine Love. If your heart resonates with that idea, you may find great comfort that the goodness of the universe supports you. Also, you would likely *feel renewed* after a session of meditating, praying and/or walking in a park.

2. Erase the ego

A number of authors would suggest that we cannot "erase the ego—that part of us that feels small and vulnerable." Some people recognize that the ego is made of fear.

Consider that you can erase the tyranny of the ego *in the moment.* How? Choose your next thought. The first thought may automatically arise from your ego. But you can pre-condition yourself to think an empowering thought as the *next thought.*

For example, I know someone who has buckets full of compassion for pets and a teaspoon full of compassion for people. My first train of thought is: "This is wrong. People are important. I'd like to see compassion shown for me and my troubles."

My *second train of thought* that I have pre-chosen is: "It is as it is. This person is different. I do not run this show."

Do you see how my second train of thought can calm me down and release me from the strain of my first thoughts' judgmental properties?

By pre-planning my second train of thought, I am free to go on and enjoy the rest of my day.

3. Engage

I'm writing a musical in which one character drops people when they become *inconvenient* to her. By this pattern, she cannot know real love because love involves supporting others even when you're in discomfort. Love is not where you go to get; it's where you go *to give.*

To experience the blessing of love, you need to *engage* in loving actions.

I have thought a lot about compassion which is part of love.

If you want other people to be happy,
practice compassion.
If you want to be happy,
practice compassion." – The Dalai Lama

And I realized that a number of people fail to practice compassion because it hurts.

It is taking on another person's hurt to some extent.

When I hear of some tragedy that a person is suffering, I sometimes reply, "I grieve with you." Pain often results from loss. So I'm acknowledging the person's loss.

I pause and pay attention. I allow myself to feel empathy.

I know some people who are too quick to offer some facile solution with thoughtless comments like: "You're young. You'll find another husband." The person offering this comment has *failed to engage*—they have failed to be truly present for the other person.

I invite you to *engage in the moment*. Be present with people. Allow yourself to feel empathy. You'll experience a new level of connection.

In summary, remember to SEE:
- Source daily by Divine Love
- Erase the ego
- Engage

As an Executive Coach, I work in a truly intuitive way. I'll ask questions in the moment that will bring up something that may surprise a client. Still, he or she will then reply with something that surprises the person. Our truth just awaits our inquiry.

Here is the truth: Your value is beyond any accomplishment or others' approval.

Your value is recognized by your Divine Source.

Connect with your Divine Source and feel a level of peace and happiness beyond the petty human conundrums of daily life.

How can you connect often with your Divine Source? What do you long for? Write down below what you would like in terms of comfort and support. Consider using prayer time or meditation time to connect with your

Divine Source.

_____

_____

_____

_____

_____

_____

_____

_____

A FINAL WORD AND
SPRINGBOARD TO YOUR DREAMS

Congratulations on your efforts as your worked with the material in this book. To get even more value from this book, take the plans and insights that you created and place them in some form in your calendar or day planner. *Plan and take action.* Return to these pages again and again to reconnect with the material and take your life to higher levels.

This section is a Springboard to Your Dreams in that I'm now sharing with you a **Method to Maximize Your Progress:** *Replace Standard Goal setting with 3 Levels Goal-setting.*

Want to avoid a standard point where people get stuck? It's in ordinary—and ineffective—goal setting.

"I hate goal setting," my friend Mitch said.

"Why?" I asked.

"First, I don't know what to write. Second, what if I fail to achieve the goal? That hurts like hell," Mitch concluded.

Goal setting can be rife with pitfalls. A goal that is too minor fails to motivate. A goal that is too lofty brings up all kinds of subconscious baggage and can torpedo your efforts.

Here's the solution: It's what I call *3 Levels Goal-setting.*

In *3 Levels Goal-Setting*, you set three levels of goals: Good, Excellent and Amazing!

Some people get stuck. They do not want to set goals that are too lofty because the fear of disappointment is too daunting.

"How can I live with failing to hit my goal?" my client Serena asked (sort of echoing Mitch's objection).

"When you use *3 Levels Goal-Setting*, you'll be able to work with such concerns," I replied.

First, you set a "reasonable and good goal." And then you can expand your thinking.

Here's an example:

- Good – Sell 30 ebooks per month
- Excellent – Sell 300 ebooks per month
- Amazing! – Sell 3,000 ebooks per month

(The reasonable goal or "Good Goal" takes the pressure off. At least, you've set an attainable goal.)

Setting an Amazing! Goal requires that you expand your thinking. And that's great!

Often, we realize that to achieve an Amazing! Goal, we need to engage the help of other people. For example, an author who wants to sell 3,000 books would do well by connecting with other authors.

The process is: Have a book launch in which other authors make an announcement to their personal esubscribers lists.

One has each author offer a gift (often a downloadable audio program), which then brings more people to the individual author's website. One gathers 15 authors with esubscribers lists of 10,000 each. That's 150,000 people reached. With 2% buying one's book, that's 3,000 copies purchased.

Now it's your turn.

Pick a goal and write down your ideas on the 3 Levels:

Your Goal – GOOD outcome

_____

_____

Your Goal – EXCELLENT outcome

Your Goal – AMAZING! outcome

Use the above *Method to Maximize Your Progress* again and again.

"Replace worry with action." – Steve Chandler

I've found setting goals and taking action to be an excellent process to relieve stress.

For example, Michael Eisner, former CEO of The Walt Disney Company, talked of an extreme health situation he endured. He said that once the plan was in place for his having quadruple bypass surgery that he was much relieved. All that was left was to have the surgery and go through the recovery process. Step by step.

This makes sense in light of how many of us feel better once a plan is in place.

To achieve extraordinary results, be sure to expand your thinking through the *3 Levels Goal-setting* process.

Set 3 Levels of Goals, refine your plans and take daily action.

The best to you,

Tom

Tom Marcoux
Executive Coach - Spoken Word Strategist

EXCERPT FROM
BE HEARD AND BE TRUSTED:
HOW YOU CAN USE SECRETS OF THE
GREATEST COMMUNICATORS
TO GET WHAT YOU WANT

3rd Edition by Tom Marcoux,
Executive Coach – Spoken Word Strategist

Table of Contents

* * * * * *

Part I, Section 1
How You Can Radiate Charisma
and Get What You Want

What terrific things could be in your life if you were charismatic?

Imagine if you could easily gain people's agreement and cooperation. Top professionals come across as charismatic. *The American Heritage Dictionary* defines "charisma" as "personal magnetism or charm."

A charismatic person makes each of us feel like the most important person in the room. How is this done? The charismatic person listens to others and connects with their pain.

A charismatic person often uses an effective story to engage people's emotions and open listeners to benevolent influence.

A charismatic person expresses compelling messages. Dictionary.com defines "compelling" as "to force or drive, especially to a course of action … to overpower … to have a powerful and irresistible effect, influence." We want to overpower inertia, low moods, and procrastination. We want to take action consistently to create the best possible situations in our own lives.

An interviewer said to me, "I'm not comfortable with the idea of 'force.'"

"All right, let's focus on having a good intention first," I replied. "Instead of force, let's aim to 'move' a person's emotions. "For example, when I was ten years old, my piano teacher knew how to persuade me to practice. She helped me see how much I improved when I practiced. She moved my emotions so that I could feel and enjoy the benefits I was getting. She also cleverly had me practice a song that I really wanted to play."

In essence, my piano teacher was a compelling communicator. She was heard and trusted by me. And that's what you'll learn how to do in this book.

How much would your life improve if you could easily get people to say yes to you? What if you could easily get them to want to say yes?

- "Yes! You're hired. The job is yours."
- "Yes! Here's your raise and promotion."
- "Yes! I'll marry you."
- "Yes! Here's $200,000 to develop your entrepreneurial idea."
- "Yes! I'll buy your product."

What if you could get what you really want – faster than you ever imagined?

That was both the opportunity and the problem for my client Sarah. She confessed, "I need to improve my communication skills."

"How would that give you what you really want?" I asked.

For a moment, she frowned in thought.

"And what do you really want?"

"A raise and a promotion!" she said with sudden clarity.

"What would that take?"

"My boss would have to trust me with higher profile assignments."

In essence, Sarah didn't just want to improve her communication skills; she wanted to be heard and be trusted.

With my guidance, Sarah learned to use the skills found in this book. She learned methods to increase her confidence, speak well to authority, and feel higher self-esteem.

For 26 years, I have helped thousands of clients and audience members become great communicators. In fact, an earlier version of this book was accepted as a textbook by Cogswell Polytechnical College and included in that college's time capsule.

The capsule is set to be opened in 2100. Even in 2100, the timeless principles of warm and trustworthy communication will be valuable.

In this book, we will cover story after story that highlight how many, including twelve billionaires and millionaires, communicate successfully to make things happen. You will also learn directly from the articles and comments of a number of other great communicators.

This book is filled with principles that can help you relate to people on a higher level of connection and cooperation.

As to methods there may be a million and then some, but principles are few. The man who grasps principles can successfully select his own methods. The man who tries methods, ignoring principles, is sure to have trouble. - Ralph Waldo Emerson

For compelling communication, you need to do two things:
1. Seize the attention
2. Create a connection

We want our communication to be not merely pleasant, but compelling. We want people to cooperate with us, to take action in the direction we're proposing. To help you make this year the best year of your life so far, we will explore the C.O.M.P.E.L. process.

C - Connect with the listener's pain
O - Open with genuineness
M - Maximize leverage
P - Pull with a story
E - Ease
L - Lift

"Be so good – they can't ignore you," said writer-actor-comedian Steve Martin in response to the question, "How do you gain big success?" With this book, you will become so good at influencing people. And, I will add, be so trustworthy that they want to do for you.

Let's move on. Let's learn how to be charismatic and influential …

Connect with the Listener's Pain

Where does it hurt? Did your attention go to your body? Did you feel tension in your neck area?

To make your message compelling, you need to uncover

your listener's pain.

Ask someone what he or she wants. The easiest way for the person to reply is to say, "What I don't want is to stay in this job.

Here's what I do not like in my current situation." The person talks about what causes pain.

What I have in my heart must come out; that is the reason I compose. - Ludwig van Beethoven

Beethoven reminds us that what is in our hearts must come out. Similarly, as great communicators we need to help our listener express his or her heartfelt pains and desires. By helping your listener identify "where it hurts," you can help her achieve a transformation.

The power of transformation reminds me of the journey of Gay Hendricks, the bestselling author of *Five Wishes* and cofounder of The Hendricks Institute. Years ago, when he was a 300-pound tobacco addict in a horrible marriage, he felt the need to reinvent himself. He says that what sustained him was a deep inner knowledge of where he was going – toward a life of soul awareness and creative fulfillment. Today he has a fit,

180-pound frame, over six feet tall. Gay was blocked. His blockage was made of conflicted feelings: he couldn't decide whether to continue studying in the University of New Hampshire counseling program or follow his desire to be a writer. Dwight Webb, an insightful professor of his, suggested, "Why not write about counseling?" Was there any reason Gay could not put his feelings and inner experiences into poems and articles connected with his profession? The answer was that he could do both things he loved. He could pursue psychological counseling and writing. Gay's poems were published in counseling journals and caught the eye of a professor at Stanford University, who helped Gay gain a fellowship to that institution for his doctorate. Gay went on to a 25-year academic career and wrote over 20 books.

When I contacted Gay a while ago, I discovered that he had found fulfillment as a screenwriter-filmmaker and as a seminar leader through The Hendricks Institute. Gay's journey shows that it is an "and" universe, not a "this or that" universe. The point is that Gay's professor Dwight Webb provided great coaching. He listened to Gay's pain and shared a new way to view the situation.

The only service a friend can really render is to keep up your courage by holding up to you a mirror in which you can see a noble image of yourself. - George Bernard Shaw

When you really want to be heard and be trusted, focus on something that will benefit the other person. Be the person's friend. Take the appropriate actions to help him or her.

With a number of my clients, we focus on the transition from novice salesperson to coach-to-action. As George Bernard Shaw points out, you as the coach can hold a friendly mirror up to your listener, who will then be able to see a noble image of the self. This noble image can inspire the listener to agree to whatever you're offering. And as the coach, you can help the person enjoy more in life and work.

It is above all by the imagination that we achieve perception and compassion and hope. - Ursula LeGuin

First, connect with the listener's pain. Then, with the knowledge you have gained, you can focus on helping. You can help people imagine a better personal future.

People in general are starved for the experience of being heard. - Gordon Livingston, M.D.

Get what you want by giving people what they crave: to be heard.

Principle:
Connect with the listener's pain and show that you have the remedy.

Power Question:
How can you gently ask questions that allow you to identify the listener's pain?*

*NOTE: * To get the maximum benefit from this book, devote at least 20 seconds to writing down the answer to each Power Question in your personal journal.*

Open with Genuineness

When you are content to be simply yourself and don't compare or compete, everybody will respect you. - Lao-tzu

"We don't need you to be perfect; we need you to be genuine," I say to my graduate students who seek to be better public speakers and pitch-givers.

Do what you said you were going to do,
when you said you were going to do it,
in exactly the way you said you were going to do it.
You won't ever get any better business advice than that.

Be there when you said you would be there.
Deliver when you said you would deliver.
Call when you said you would call.
Be a person who can be counted on
by keeping his word every time.
- Larry Winget

Have you ever been afraid that when you are giving a speech, your mind might go blank or you might lose your place? The solution is, *be genuine.*

When I coach CEOs and company presidents in how to give speeches, I help them express genuineness. This helps the CEO connect with the audience and motivate team members.

End of Excerpt from
Be Heard and Be Trusted: How You Can Use Secrets of the Greatest Communicators to Get What You Want
Copyright Tom Marcoux Media, LLC

Purchase your copy of this book (paperback or ebook) at Amazon.com or BarnesandNoble.com
See **Free Chapters** of Tom Marcoux's 28 books
at http://amzn.to/ZiCTRj

ABOUT THE AUTHOR

Tom Marcoux helps people like you fulfill big dreams. Known as an **Executive Coach - Spoken Word Strategist** and TFG Thought Leader, Tom has authored 28 books with sales in 15 countries. One of his *Darkest Secrets* books rose to #1 on Amazon.com Hot New Releases in Business Life (and in Business Communication). He guides clients and audiences (IBM, Sun Microsystems, etc.) to success in leadership, team building, job interviewing, public speaking, media relations, and branding. A member of the National Speakers Association, he is a professional coach and guest expert on TV, radio, and print, and was dubbed "the Personal Branding Instructor" by the *San Francisco Examiner.*

Tom addressed National Association of Broadcasters' Conference six years running. With a degree in psychology, Tom is a guest lecturer at **Stanford University**, DeAnza, & California State University, and teaches business communication, designing careers, public speaking, science fiction cinema/literature and comparative religion at Academy of Art University. Winner of a special award at the **Emmys**, Tom wrote, directed, and produced a feature film that the distributor took to the **Cannes film market**, and the film gained international distribution. He is engaged in book/film projects *Crystal Pegasus* (children's) and *TimePulse* (science fiction). See TomSuperCoach.com and Tom's well-received blog

at www.BeHeardandBeTrusted.com

Consider engaging **Tom Marcoux as your Executive Coach.**

"As Tom's client for many years, I have benefited from

his wisdom and strategic approach. Do your career and personal life a big favor and get his books and engage him as **your Executive Coach**." – Dr. JoAnn Dahlkoetter, author, Your Performing Edge and to CEOs & Olympic Gold Medalists

Tom Marcoux can help you with **speech writing** and **coaching for your best performance.**

As Tom says, *Make Your Speech a Pleasant Beach.*

Join Tom's Linkedin.com group: *Executive Public Speaking and Communication Power.*

At Google+: join the community "Create Your Best Life – Charisma & Confidence"

Get a **Free** report: "9 Deadly Mistakes to Avoid for Your Next Speech and 9 Surefire Methods" at

http://tomsupercoach.com/freereport9Mistakes4Speech.html

Tom Marcoux has trained CEOs, small business owners, and graduate students to speak with impact and gain audiences' tremendous approval and cooperation. *Learn how to present and get thunderous applause!*

"Tom, Thanks for your coaching and work with me on revising my speech at a major university. Working with you has been so enlightening for me. Through your gentle prodding and guidance I was able to write a speech that connects with the audience. I wish everyone could experience the transformation I have undergone. You have helped me discover the warm and compelling stories that now make my speech reach hearts and uplift minds. This was truly an empowering experience. I cannot thank you enough for your great assistance." — J.S.

"Tom Marcoux has been an NAB Conference favorite [speaker] for six years. And he is very energetic."
– John Marino,
Vice President, National Association of Broadcasters, Washington, D.C.

"Using just one of Tom Marcoux's methods, I got more done in 2 weeks than in 6 months."
– Jaclyn Freitas, M.A.

Tom's Coaching features innovations:
- Dynamic Rehearsal
- Power Rehearsal for Crisis
- The Charisma Advantage that Saves Time

Become a fan of Tom's graphic novels/feature films:
Fantasy Thriller: *Jack AngelSword*
type "JackAngelSword" at Facebook.com

Science fiction: *TimePulse*
www.facebook.com/timepulsegraphicnovel

Children's Fantasy: *Crystal Pegasus*
www.facebook.com/crystalpegasusandrose

See **Free Chapters** of Tom Marcoux's 28 books
at http://amzn.to/ZiCTRj

Special Offer Just for Readers of this Book:

Contact Tom Marcoux at tomsupercoach@gmail.com for special discounts on books, coaching, workshops and presentations. Just mention your experience with this book.

Your Notes:

_____

_____

_____

_____

_____

_____

_____

_____